SPORT'S GREATEST STATISTICAL ANOMALIES

James Salmon

First published by Ultimate World Publishing 2022
Copyright © 2022 James Salmon

ISBN

Paperback: 978-1-922828-87-3
Ebook: 978-1-922828-88-0

James Salmon has asserted his rights under the Copyright, Designs and Patents Act 1988 to be identified as the author of this work. The information in this book is based on the author's experiences and opinions. The publisher specifically disclaims responsibility for any adverse consequences which may result from use of the information contained herein. Permission to use information has been sought by the author. Any breaches will be rectified in further editions of the book.

All rights reserved. No part of this publication may be reproduced, stored in or introduced into a retrieval system, or transmitted in any form, or by any means (electronic, mechanical, photocopying, recording or otherwise) without the prior written permission of the author. Any person who does any unauthorised act in relation to this publication may be liable to criminal prosecution and civil claims for damages. Enquiries should be made through the publisher.

Cover design: Ultimate World Publishing
Layout and typesetting: Ultimate World Publishing
Editor: James Salmon
Cover Image Copyright: 3d_kot-Shutterstock.com

Ultimate World Publishing
Diamond Creek,
Victoria Australia 3089
www.writeabook.com.au

Dedication

To my friends and family, without whose persistent pestering about whether I was ever going to actually finish this book, I might never have actually finished this book.

Contents

	Dedication	iii
	Prologue	1
1	Basketball Season: Wilt Chamberlain, 1961/62	3
2	Surfing Career: Kelly Slater	13
3	Cricket Team: The West Indies, 1980s and '90s	25
4	Tennis Event: John Isner vs Nicolas Mahut	39
5	Tennis Event: Vicki Nelson v Jean Hepner	47
6	Swimming Career: Michael Phelps	49
7	Golf Career: Tiger Woods	57
8	Cricket Career: Don Bradman	73
9	Basketball Career: John Stockton	87
10	Tennis Careers: The Big Three (Rafael Nadal, Novak Djokovic, Roger Federer)	99
11	Soccer Team: Leicester City, 2015	111
12	Golf Season: Byron Nelson, 1945	121
13	Ice Hockey Career: Wayne Gretzky	131
14	Squash Career: Heather McKay	141
15	Basketball Team: The Boston Celtics, 1950s and '60s	151
	About the Author	161

Prologue

STATISTICAL ANOMALIES IS a phrase which elicits vastly different responses in different people. To some – arguably the majority – that response is an eyeroll and a rapid switching off of the brain. To others, perhaps a rarer breed, anomalies are a fascinating phenomenon.

For me, sporting anomalies in particular have always been a source of keen interest. As a sports-mad kid, Don Bradman was the first outlier to grab my attention. Despite retiring from cricket before my parents were born, his dumbfounding stats lived on in the minds of many Australians and – for me – through my incessant chatter in the back of my parents' car, in the school yard and at my first sleepovers.

I felt like I had discovered something for myself – how could one person deviate so far from the pack? I had to spread the word.

I devoured the stats like a kid eating his one tuck shop lunch for the week, and regurgitated the stories which had been passed down the generations to any poor soul polite enough to listen. And as I got older, my appetite for anomalies only grew.

At 18 years of age, I recall following the John Isner vs Nicolas Mahut match at Wimbledon, gradually realising the enormity of what was unfolding on the other side of the world. Then in 2015, along came

Leicester City. I've passionately followed a wide assortment of sports over my 30 years, but soccer is one to which I haven't typically devoted much time. Despite that, I was captivated by Leicester's unlikely Premier League triumph in 2015, with the incredible tale of the underdog drawing me in from the sidelines.

Such unlikely events have the power to turn a passive bystander into the most fervent fan. And, given the plethora of similarly improbable sporting occurrences stowed away in the recesses of my brain, coupled with my actual job as a sportswriter, this provided the perfect excuse to combine business with pleasure.

So here we are. If you're like me and love sports and numbers, then hopefully you'll enjoy me rambling on about them over the course of these next couple of hundred pages. If not, perhaps the levity I've tried to incorporate alongside the facts, figures and graphs (all 28 of them) will at least elicit a laugh or two from you along the way.

It's worth noting that, much to my chagrin, stats and records do have the habit of changing over time. Most chapters in this book didn't pose much of a problem in this regard – Byron Nelson isn't winning any more PGA tournaments in 1945, nor will anyone go close to matching him – but a couple needed update after update. The Big Three chapter was one example, with the tennis world rudely continuing to play Grand Slams as I fine-tuned my prose. Steph Gilmore's eighth world title in 2022, one of the most memorable moments in the history of professional surfing, was also highly inconvenient for me and my Kelly Slater chapter.

But alas, at some point I needed to actually publish the book and accept that a handful of the numbers might change. All figures are up-to-date as of September 2022 so buckle up and enjoy the ride before those chapters are rendered obsolete!

1

Basketball Season: Wilt Chamberlain, 1961/62

IN BASKETBALL, IT'S good to be tall. In fact, barring the extremely talented, it's something of a prerequisite. Watch a modern-day NBA game and you often won't see a player on the court under the size of 6'3" or 6'4" (190cm+). LeBron James has been running around at 6'9", or 206cm, for a couple of decades, and his height is probably not even his defining athletic quality. The same could be said for Giannis Antetokounmpo, who came along at a tick under 7'0" (211cm) and with each arm the size of an entire regular-sized person. The things these players can do at their height is hard to believe, and puts to shame the athletic gifts of many extraordinary players in other sports around the world.

But this wasn't always the case. As a species we've grown taller by the generation, so it's not surprising that the same can be said for basketball players. Rewind half a century and, while the average NBA player would still have been an imposing specimen in 2022, they typically weren't at the same level as those we see today.

Wilt Chamberlain was anything but typical. A hugely impressive athlete from a young age, Chamberlain entered the NBA in 1959 and proceeded to smash records like they were going out of fashion, many of which still stand today. He dominated the league from the outset, and any book dedicated to statistical anomalies in sport worth its salt needs a chapter dedicated to him.

Looking at Wilt as an anomaly could take many angles. His single-game scoring record of 100 points is anomalous enough in itself, his rebounding numbers are bizarre – though somewhat less anomalous given Bill Russell's existence – and some of his points records need to be seen to be believed. His 1961/62 season was the piece de resistance of his career, at least from a statistical perspective, and it's in his season-long averages that year that he earned his place in this book – presumably one of his driving motivations.

Chamberlain entered the NBA after a decorated high school and college career. Standing at 7'1", or 216cm, he didn't waste any time making an impact, averaging 37.6 points and 27 rebounds in his rookie season. For reference, this 37.6-point average is already higher than what any other player has ever managed in the history of the game, and is only bested by three of Wilt's own seasons. The same goes for the 27 rebounds – the only single season in which a player averaged more was 1960/61, Wilt's second year, when he averaged 27.2.

At the time the most highly paid player in NBA history, Wilt took things to the next level in his third season. He kicked things off with 40+ point/20+ rebound games in nine of his first ten outings, and would ultimately go on to average 50.4 points, 25.7 rebounds and a couple of assists per game over the course of the season. Anyone who follows basketball would see those numbers and laugh – 50-point games typically come along every few weeks as a one-off occurrence and are a worthy talking point even as a standalone figure, while 25-rebound efforts are even more rare. To average these over a close-to-100 game season is seemingly impossible.

Though he put up absurd numbers virtually every night that season, a couple in particular stand out. On the 8th of December, the Warriors played a triple-overtime game against the Lakers. Wilt, who didn't spend a solitary second on the bench all season, played 63 minutes as a result, and accumulated 78 points and 43 rebounds. He did this despite missing 15 free throws, and his Warriors still lost by four points. A month later he had a 73-point/36-rebound night against the Chicago Packers – that one he managed in a regular 48 minutes. There are games in which entire teams barely surpass these numbers in the modern-day NBA.

Today's NBA media has developed an at times annoying habit of glorifying individual achievements by lauding a player as the first to ever do something very specific. For example, you might hear that Player X is the first in the history of the game to average at least 17 points, 17 rebounds and 3.2 assists over eight consecutive games. It wouldn't matter if someone else had averaged 30 points, 16.8 rebounds and ten assists over 30 consecutive games, because that doesn't fit into the criteria, even though it's far more impressive. If the media in the '60s was anything like it is today, they would have had a field day with Wilt's numbers. I think we can safely assume that these games – let's categorise them as 70+-point/35+-rebound nights – would require very little statistical manipulation to find them a category of their own.

But these weren't even his biggest nights of the year – that came in the fifth last game of the regular season. His Warriors took on the Knicks, and Wilt went 36-63 from the field and 28-32 from the line to score the first (and to this date only) ever 100-point game in the

NBA, while also grabbing 25 rebounds. Scoring was a little different back then, but in today's game those numbers could feasibly mean that he stole almost all of the available stats in the match.

Evidently, Wilt accumulated buckets with an ease which has probably never been matched. At 7'1", in today's game he would have been a slightly taller than average centre, but back in the '60s he often stood head and shoulders (or, in a literal sense, probably just head) above the rest. In his 100-point game, the 6'10" (or 208cm) Darrall Imhoff started at centre, and likely guarded (or tried to guard) Chamberlain for much of the 20 minutes that he was on the floor, while the 6'9" (206cm) Cleveland Buckner took care of the rest. This wasn't always the case and there were some guys in the league at the time who pushed the 7'0" mark, but that kind of height combined with the athleticism possessed by Wilt is something much more synonymous with today's era than with the '60s.

With this in mind, it will come as no surprise to you to learn that long before Chamberlain became the most prolific scorer in NBA history, he was a prodigious athlete. Basketball didn't particularly interest him at a young age; instead, he was a talented high jumper, long jumper, shot putter and track runner. After reaching 6'0" by the age of ten, however, and 6'11" by the beginning of high school, it was inevitable that he would turn to basketball – something which turned out to be a wise choice. What kind of a career he would have had as an athlete is pure speculation, but unless he could run 100 metres in around seven seconds, it's unlikely he would have reached the statistical heights on the track that he did on the basketball court.

He was also the catalyst for a couple of significant rule changes which still exist in the game today. Rumour has it he used to dunk his free throws – which would ultimately become one of the few weaknesses in his game – and it's for that reason that the NCAA (the governing body for college sports in America) banned the practice. It was around the same time that they banned offensive goaltending, with Wilt supposedly a major factor in that as well.

But not even those rule changes could stop him. The mind boggles at the thought of what he could have averaged had he been allowed to dunk free throws and offensive goaltending wasn't outlawed, but he managed to put up some fairly decent numbers regardless, and the below graphs demonstrate just how statistically dominant he was. While Chamberlain's third season at the top level was where he really planted his name in the record books, numerous seasons throughout his career stick out like Wilt himself at a party of normal-sized people.

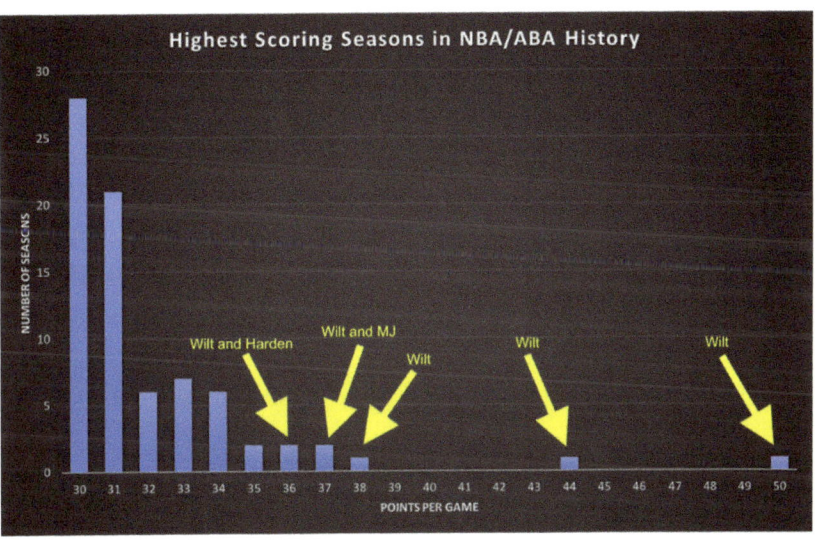

Included in the above graph is every season in NBA/ABA history up until 2022 in which a player averaged 30 or more points (the ABA being the league with which the NBA merged in 1976). When a player averaged between 30 and 31 points throughout a season they are included in the 30-point category, where there are 28 cases, while seasons in which a player averaged between 31 and 32 points are included in the 31-point category, and so on. I chose 30 as a starting point completely arbitrarily because it's a lot and it's a rounded number, but regardless of where you start Chamberlain's dominance is plain to see. His 1961/62 season, of course, is way out there on its own, while his '62/63 season would probably also be worthy of a place in this book itself were it not for Wilt's season prior. He also owns the third bar on the graph, while of the four other seasons with a scoring average of over 36, two belong to him.

He doesn't stand out quite as much in the following graph detailing the highest rebounding averages in NBA/ABA history, but as I mentioned earlier, if Bill Russell was never around it would be a different story. Wilt owns all three of the seasons in which a player had a rebounding average in excess of 25, while of the next 15, six belong to him and nine to Russell. The highest rebounding average in a season by someone not called Wilt Chamberlain or Bill Russell belongs to Nate Thurmond. Nate the Great, as he is affectionately known, managed 21.26 in 1966/67, bringing him in at 19th on the list.

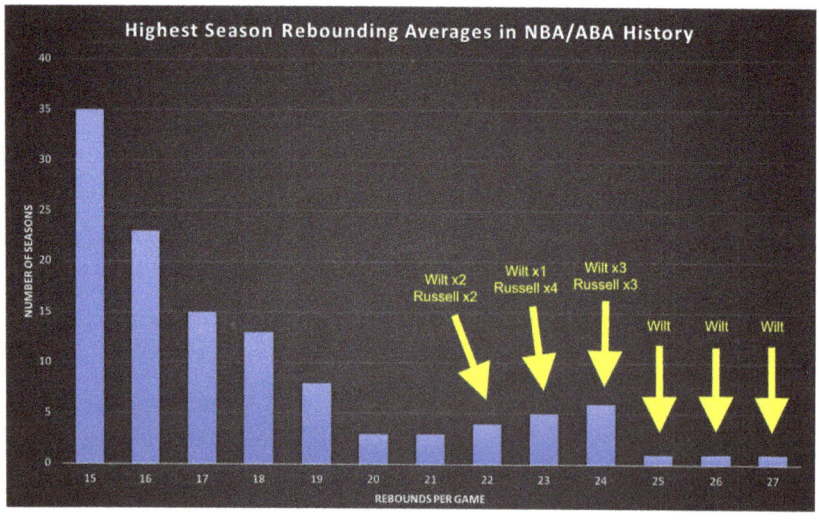

BASKETBALL SEASON: WILT CHAMBERLAIN, 1961/62

Clearly Wilt's height, athleticism, and a fair old chunk of natural talent were the underlying reasons for his dominance, but there were a couple of other factors contributing to his anomalous statistics. The first of these is that he literally never went to the bench. In his 1961/62 season he played every single second of all 92 games that his Philadelphia Warriors played. Today's game isn't quite the same story. As an example, Pascal Siakam and Fred VanVleet ended the 2021/22 regular season sharing the lead for minutes per game, and they sat at 37.9 per night – less than 80% of the game. Obviously having an extra ten minutes per game helps you to rack up some extra statistics – not as many as Wilt did, but certainly a few more. In fact, Wilt's numbers from that season per 36 minutes – a common statistical measure used in today's game – were 37.4 points, 19 rebounds and 1.8 assists. These are still crazy numbers, but obviously don't indicate quite the level of dominance that his per game stats do.

He also took an absurd number of shots. Basketball is a funny game in that, theoretically, I could go out on an NBA court and score a few points just by shooting every time I touched the ball. The only problem is that I would be horribly inefficient and my team would lose by 100 points. Wilt wasn't horribly inefficient by any stretch of the imagination, but he did take nearly 40 shots per game in 1961/62. For comparison, the field goal attempts leader in the 2021/22 season was Luka Dončić with 21.6 per game. Dončić wouldn't take 40 shots per night because his efficiency would likely drop significantly from the 45.7% it was at that season, but Chamberlain could justify it because he still scored on over 50% of his attempts. As a result, it was probably reasonable for him to take a lot of shots, but it certainly makes it easier to have such a dominant scoring season when you're getting 40 looks a night.

Another mitigating factor is the relative ease with which teams scored in Wilt's era. His Philadelphia Warriors averaged 125.44

points per game during the 1961/62 regular season, almost ten more than the highest scoring team in 2021/22 and close to 15 points higher than the average team that year. This difference isn't *enormous* and can to an extent be explained by the scoring of Wilt himself, but it is a difference nonetheless. There were also a number of games throughout the season which would be completely out of place in the modern-day NBA – as an example, his Warriors beat the Knicks 169-147 in his 100-point game. Nowadays, that kind of scoring is reserved for the All-Star game, an exhibition in which almost literally no defence is played.

In fact, if we use these factors to extrapolate the numbers of current players, there are a few who would go close to matching Wilt's achievements. James Harden, for example, had one of the most prodigious scoring seasons in history in 2018/19 when he averaged 36.1 points in 36.8 minutes. If he played 48 minutes per game scoring at this rate he would have averaged 47.09 points. Factor in the difference in scoring between the '61/62 Warriors and Harden's '18/19 Rockets and that number goes up to 51.86.

Of course, this is an imperfect comparison and there are other mitigating factors to be considered. Harden, for example, took 13.2 3-point attempts per game in the aforementioned season. The 3-point line didn't exist during Chamberlain's first ten seasons, and if the statistics are to be believed he never attempted one when it was introduced.

Regardless, there are certainly some factors at play which help to explain how he managed to put up such anomalous numbers. But they don't diminish the achievements – there were plenty of other guys in the league at the same time and none of them managed 50-point/25-rebound seasons, so Wilt is still well and truly worthy of the adulation these numbers bring him.

Criticisms of Chamberlain exist to this day, predominantly centred around the fact that he *only* won two NBA titles – an unsurprising slight given the success-driven narrative with which the NBA world is so obsessed. Comparisons between he and Bill Russell are often drawn given they were the two dominant players of that era, and Russell is regularly given the nod due to his supposed superior ability to make his team better – and fair enough, too, given that is the ultimate goal of team sports. Indeed, it was Russell who took the league MVP from Wilt in 1962 despite averaging more than 33 points less and relatively similar numbers in the other major statistical categories.

Whether these criticisms are valid, however, is a question for another day, or another book. What is unequivocal is that Chamberlain's numbers defied belief, both in the era in which he achieved them and today. They will almost certainly never be matched, and his 1961/62 season will likely forever standalone as one of the greatest statistical outliers in sporting history.

By the Numbers

- Chamberlain's **50.36 points per game** in the 1961/62 season is **13.27 more points per game** than any player (excluding Chamberlain himself) has managed in history, with **Michael Jordan's 37.09 ppg** in 1986/87 the next best.

- Chamberlain is the owner of the **top 4 seasons** in NBA/ABA history in terms of points per game, as well as **5 of the top 6 and 7 of the top 19**.

- Chamberlain is the **only player to score 100 points in a single game**, which he did during the aforementioned 1961/62 season; in **second place is Kobe Bryant with 81**. Chamberlain also **scored 78, 73 on 2 occasions, and 72** during that season and the next, numbers which only Bryant and David Thompson (73 points in 1978) have ever matched.

- Chamberlain **exceeded an average of 22 rebounds per game in 9 seasons** throughout his career. **Bill Russell is his only peer in this regard**, matching those 9 seasons in excess of 22 rpg; **no other player has ever done it even once**.

2

Surfing Career: Kelly Slater

JOHNNY UTAH. THE word 'stoked'. Coronas. For most people around the world, these are the things that come to mind when surfing is mentioned. Even though it's enjoyed on a global scale, it's still a relatively niche sport, and the professional side of it is even more so.

Estimates vary enormously on how many people actually surf around the world – a report by *Transworld Business* in 2015 put it at around 2.7 million, while a couple of years later the International Surfing Association put that number at up to 35 million, which tells us that a) either one or both of those studies are completely inaccurate, and b) it's safe to say that surfers make up a fairly small (and very localised) percentage of the global population. In contrast, soccer was estimated to have 265 million participants when FIFA did their 'Big Count' survey back in 2006, and given that was 23 million more than in 2000 that number has probably grown to well over 300 million by now.

And that's just participants. While most major sports have a lot more fans than players, it's safe to assume that surfing is the opposite. One reason for this assumption is simply that surfing is something you can do for most of your life, so participation estimates take into account people of all ages, while in other sports the players tend to be on the younger side of the scale. Fans, however, can remain fans until the day they die. On top of that, I would fathom a guess that unlike with other sports, there are very few avid fans of professional surfing who don't actually surf themselves, and among those who do surf there are plenty who don't care for the World Surf League. Because surfing isn't about competition, man – it's a lifestyle.

Despite all that, Kelly Slater is a household name. He's as well-known as most celebrated athletes around the globe, even though he reached the heights of his fame through a less popular medium. Among the surfing community it's pretty widely understood why, but the actual statistics might have eluded the less gnarly among you: unequivocally the greatest surfer the world has ever seen, Slater has accumulated an astonishing 11 world titles. The next most is eight, by Australian Stephanie Gilmore, while the second most on the male's side is only (only being a relative term) five, by Mark Richards back in the '70s and '80s.

More than twice as successful as any other male surfer in history and roughly 1.375 times more successful than any other surfer at all, he is the biggest star in the sport's history, and was the first – and probably to this date only – surfer whose fame transcended its boundaries. Slater played a major role in taking pro surfing into the mainstream. He made possible the concept of a surfer becoming famous outside the proverbial four walls of surfing – the green room, you might say – with his dominance in the water leading to boundless opportunities on land.

SURFING CAREER: KELLY SLATER

For a while he was everywhere – he tried his hand at acting, most notably playing Jimmy Slade in *Baywatch* (and ultimately going on to date Pamela Anderson), formed a band with fellow pro surfers which they very aptly called *The Surfers*, was the eponymous star of the video game *Kelly Slater's Pro Surfer,* and modelled for Versace. Unlike many star surfers before him, his fame wasn't limited to places like California, Hawaii and Australia. He was a global phenomenon.

Slater won his first world title back in 1992 and as of 2022 was still (technically) going, seemingly unable to fully commit to retirement, and incredibly in the first event of that season he turned back the clock by winning at Pipeline. By the age of 50 his best was nonetheless well and truly behind him, but even so his reign at the top stretched for close to two decades, with his last world title coming just a few months short of his 40th birthday in 2011.

Slater competed in his first full pro season at the age of 18. He struggled in both that and his second year, but in 1992 he exploded into relevance with a string of impressive performances, and courtesy of event wins first in Hossegor, France and then at the Pipe Masters in Hawaii to round out the season, he became the youngest ever world champion at the age of just 20. The next year Hawaii's Derek Ho took out his first and only world title – Kelly settled for fifth – and that would be the last time until nearly the turn of the century that somebody not named Kelly Slater would do so.

In 1994 he won in a relatively close season, and the next year scraped over the line by the barest of margins over both Rob Machado and Sunny Garcia. 1996 and 1997 saw Slater's domination peak as he cruised to victory in both years, and in 1998 he won his fifth consecutive title – incidentally the most any other male surfer has won at all, let alone in succession.

Evidently sick of winning, he then took an extended hiatus from professional surfing, not returning full-time to the tour until 2003 – a year in which he came second by a slim margin to Andy Irons, with whom he would share an intense and highly publicised rivalry.

2004 was probably Slater's worst year on the tour since 1991. Despite competing in all 11 tournaments throughout the season, he failed to win a single event and ultimately finished in third place – a long way behind Irons, who won a third consecutive title.

By this point in time, Irons had well and truly taken the crown from Kelly. He was six years younger and Slater hadn't won a world title for six years. In fairness, Slater was either absent or only competing in a handful of events for four of those, but upon his return Irons had proved to be the better surfer over the course of 2003 and 2004 – not something the hyper-competitive Slater would have taken kindly to. Many attribute this changing of the guard – particularly at the hands of the cocky Irons, one of the few competitors willing to publicly express anything remotely resembling contempt for his predecessor – as one of the primary reasons for Slater's resurgence. There's no doubt that the fire in his belly which had led him to five consecutive titles in the '90s had dimmed, and an arrogant, outspoken and extremely talented Irons helped to reignite it. But while that rivalry may certainly have played a part in the ensuing resurgence, Slater must have had a fair bit left in the tank regardless given that he had, by that point, only won a little over half of the 11 world titles he would ultimately finish with.

The rivalry continued into 2005, when the pair won six of the 11 tournaments throughout the year and finished first and second again, well ahead of a young Mick Fanning in third. This time, however, it was Kelly who got the chocolates, adding 'oldest ever world champion' to a resume which already included 'youngest ever world champion'.

For those who have lost count, this was his seventh title – already a huge number, but it's testament to his longevity that he would go on to become the oldest ever world champion on another four occasions.

The next year he proved once again that, even in his mid-30s, he was the best surfer in the world, finishing in the top five in all nine tournaments in which he competed and the top three in eight of them to take out another world title ahead of – you guessed it – Andy Irons, who was a fair way back in second place.

He missed out the next year, before returning in kind in 2008 with one of his best years yet – aged 36. He won six of the ten tournaments which he entered and finished the season with 8,832 points, miles ahead of his nearest competitor, Bede Durbidge, who had 6,780 points. His tenth world title came two years later when he finished with 69,000 points, but as you may have guessed that number was courtesy of a change in the scoring system rather than an almost nine-fold improvement. Still, second-placed Jordy Smith only had 52,250, so it was another pretty dominant year.

Kelly was nearly 40 by this stage and his whole career was getting pretty ridiculous, but he capped it off the next year by winning his 11th world title, again with relative ease. And that was it. His 11th and final title.

An obvious regression in his surfing – which could reasonably have been expected a decade earlier – still didn't really come for another few years. He could easily have added another world title or two in 2012 and 2013, years in which he finished second by slim margins to a couple of 30-something year-old Aussies named Joel Parkinson and Mick Fanning, both of whom had seen their potential career earnings significantly diminished throughout the previous decade as a result of Kelly's dominance.

A decline finally ensued thereafter, with the name Kelly Slater gradually dropping down the Championship Tour rankings over the following seasons. Injuries also began to contribute to his demise – not unexpected for a nearly-50-year-old competing in a high-intensity professional sport – and by the end of the 2010s he was flitting in and out of the tour pretty much as he pleased, turning much of his attention to extra-curricular activities – like making his own wave pool, where, in 2019, the World Surf League began holding one of their Championship Tour events.

This, perhaps more than anything, is testament to just how much of a dominant force Slater has been in the surfing world. If someone could actually own a pastime, he would own surfing. A few years earlier, the prospect of an artificial wave pool was something of a pipe dream, or perhaps more aptly in surfing vernacular, a tube dream. Not only did he help bring it into existence, but he managed to convince the powers that be that it would be more interesting to watch the world's best surfers carve around on a perfect but fake wave, rather than some of the best real waves in the world. The Surf Ranch Pro took place for the first time in 2018 at Slater's Surf Ranch in inland California, and while its first stint on the Championship Tour only lasted three years, it's still hard to imagine that anyone else would have even close to the requisite influence over the sport to make such a significant and divisive change a reality – particularly in their own pool.

With the amount of winning he did, however, it probably shouldn't be a surprise how much influence he has over the sport. The graph which you'll see below provides a visual representation of this success, showcasing his career relative to every other surfer to win a world title on the male side of professional surfing. It harks back to 1964, when Australia's Midget Farrelly won what was then called the ISF World Surfing Championships, the first organised, global

SURFING CAREER: KELLY SLATER

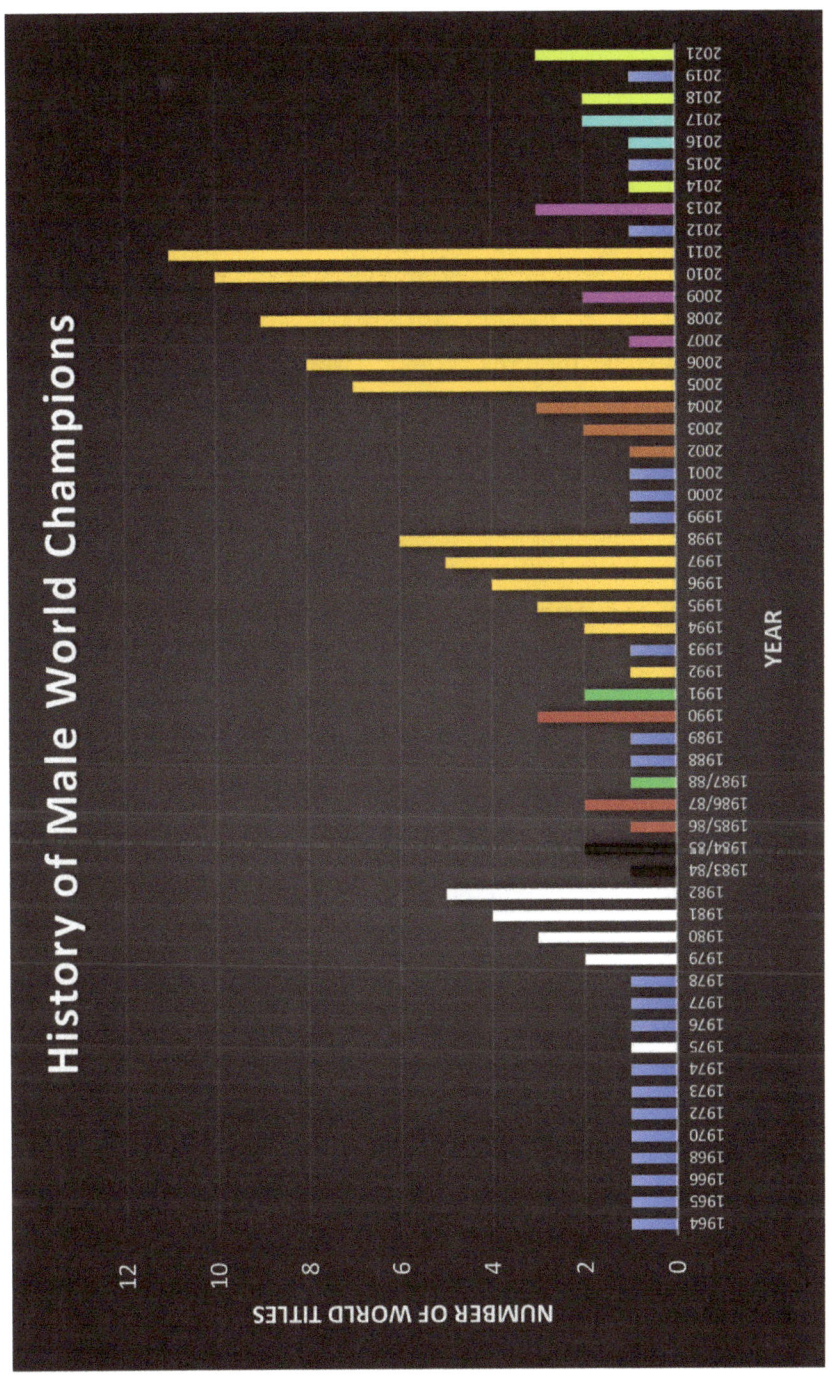

surfing championship in the sport's history. The bar for each year thereafter demonstrates how many world titles that year's champion had won to that point in their career, and Kelly assembles his tower like an obnoxious architect trying to build the world's biggest building in a city with no other high rises.

The blue bars represent every world champion who won only a solitary title in their careers. Surfers who won on more than one occasion each have their own colour – Mark Richards, for example, who won in 1975, 1979, 1980, 1981 and 1982, is in white, while Mick Fanning is in violet and Andy Irons in orange. Slater, obviously, is in gold.

It's probably worth detailing at this point just how a WSL season works – what does winning a world title actually entail? Is it possible to bumble your way to a few of them without being definitively better than your opposition? Throughout the course of Slater's career, every men's season has consisted of either 10 or 11 events, each taking place at a different location around the globe. The number of competitors in each tournament has varied over the years, but typically it's between 32 and 48. There were four surfers in most heats for a large part of Slater's career, but in the latter stages of his winning years that was only the case in the early heats, and generally after the first round or two of a tournament heats were one on one, with the loser of each heat eliminated until there was just one man – often Slater – left standing.

Every finishing position in every contest is worth a certain number of points, and competitors accumulate these points over the course of the year to determine the world champion. So it's a long process to get there, and even though surfing is one of the few sports in the world in which the winner is based on subjective judging, enough competition goes on in a year that the world champion is typically a deserving one. This means we can rule out the role of luck – that the world title doesn't necessarily always go to the best-performed surfer. It almost always does, and winning it requires sustained success over the course of an entire year.

Winning a solitary world title is an enormous achievement – the peak of a professional surfer's career. So how did Kelly manage to win 11 of them when no other male has won more than five? Clearly there's a hefty dose of talent involved – that's the obvious answer. But like most dominant champions in professional sport, an unquenchable thirst for victory also played a major role.

Contrary to what might be the prevailing view among laypeople, surfing has for a long time had no shortage of surfers both professional and amateur renowned for their competitive nature in the water. From the likes of Rabbit Bartholomew making pests of themselves in Hawaii throughout the 1970s to guys like Gabriel Medina in the modern-day WSL, a killer instinct which probably seems at odds with the laidback lifestyle so synonymous with surfing is prevalent among many of these athletes.

Kelly Slater might not have always seemed as obnoxiously competitive as some in the water and he's not quite old enough to have been involved in the aforementioned power struggle in Hawaii in the '70s, but to dismiss this element of his personality is to do a disservice to his obsession with winning. He is eloquent and thoughtful enough that sometimes he can mask it in extended interviews, particularly as he's reached a more advanced age, but get him in any situation where winning is at stake and the proverbial switch is flicked. He is oft-regarded as the most competitive person in the history of pro surfing – a title for which he has some pretty stiff competition – and sounds like the type of guy who would get upset if you beat him to the breakfast table in the morning. This competitive nature has been a hallmark of his career in the water.

One medium through which this competitivity was often released was through his notorious mind games, though the man himself has regularly downplayed just how many of these he truly has stashed away. He once told an anecdote of a heat in which he watched opponent Joel Parkinson, caught between two types of turns, fall from a wave. The story goes that Joel blamed Kelly for the fall, claiming the 11-time world champion got in his head. Kelly, however, was adamant he hadn't done a thing but watch. As he said in a later interview, if his opponents thought he was playing tricks on them, he'd already won. His reputation for mind games probably didn't come from nowhere, but it also seems feasible that as his career progressed, he built so much real estate in the collective minds of his opponents that his presence alone was enough to bring them unstuck.

Very few of the greatest ever in their respective sports around the world reach the heights of fame without possessing a competitive drive which is almost impossible to understand for regular people like you and me. Kelly Slater is no exception. At the long and illustrious zenith of his career, he was as obsessed with winning as probably any other competitor in surfing history. But where others wear that aspect of their personality on their sleeve, Slater was at times able to tuck it away under his wetsuit. He has been renowned in the surfing world for his ability to get under the skin of his opponents, and despite his protests, it's no accident. Just as he always has been in his surfing, Slater was methodical in the way he released his competitive drive.

But of course, hyper-competitivity isn't enough to win more than two times as many world titles as any other male surfer in history. You also need to be pretty damn good. And pretty damn good he was.

Incredibly, Slater probably left a world title or three on the table – or, perhaps more appropriately, in the water. His extended hiatus over the turn of the century came when he was winning without breaking a sweat, and having won five on the trot prior it's safe to assume he could have snared at least a couple more between 1999 and 2002 if he so desired. The tower that he built above, his own Burj Khalifa, could easily have been even bigger.

This isn't a sporting anomaly that results from an unlikely set of circumstances, or a run of extreme luck. Kelly Slater is just one of those rare sporting phenomenons. He is an athlete who is simply far, far better than anyone else in the history of his sport, and it's hard to see that ever changing.

By the Numbers

- Slater's **11 world titles** is **3 more than any other surfer** in history, and **6 more than any other male.**

- He is both the **youngest surfer to ever win a world title** (20 years old) and the **oldest surfer to ever win a world title** (which he first did aged 33).

- After becoming the oldest surfer to win a world title, Slater went on to be crowned world champion on **another 4 occasions**.

- His final world title came at the **age of 39**.

- **20 seasons passed** between Slater's first and last world titles.

3

Cricket Team: The West Indies, 1980s and '90s

When I was a kid, the Australian Test cricket team was unstoppable. Names like Ponting, Hayden and Langer dominated the batting order, while the likes of Warne and McGrath helped make up one of the most formidable bowling line-ups of all time. We didn't really ever lose. In fact, two times before my 16th birthday, Australia enjoyed comfortably the two longest winning streaks in Test cricket history, the first of which spanned 18 months and the second of which lasted more than two years.

I remember my Year 8 teacher telling me at the time that he no longer followed cricket as he found it uninteresting. Plenty of (wrong) people believe that to be a fact in and of itself, but his reasoning wasn't an actual criticism of the game – it was simply because Australia was too good. In most matches the result was a foregone conclusion before the first ball was bowled, so he didn't think it worth his time to pay attention. As a 13-year-old, I of course found this to be ridiculous and borderline blasphemy – winning is fun, so what's the problem Mr. Williams?

As it turns out, Mr. Williams can thank his lucky stars he wasn't living in the Caribbean throughout the '80s and '90s, because if he thought watching the Australian cricket team of the early 21st century dominate was mundane, the West Indian team of a decade or two earlier might have lulled him into a permanent coma.

All cricket lovers know of their dominance. Those old enough to have enjoyed it regale us younger generations with stories about the dread they would instil in opponents and fans alike – of their seemingly endless list of terrifying fast bowlers who were more concerned with decapitating batters than getting wickets. Bowlers who, in the absence of speed guns, were apparently capable of bowling twice as fast as anyone since bowling speeds have begun to be recorded.

It's possible the passing of time has aggrandised the team, as it has a tendency to do. But a side boasting at various points Courtney Walsh, Malcolm Marshall, Joel Garner, Michael Holding, Curtly Ambrose, Colin Croft, Andy Roberts and Ian Bishop certainly sounds pretty scary – and that's just the bowlers – and their record over a pretty long period of time isn't far off mirroring what it would look like if they literally had decapitated their opposition.

The statistical anomaly that they managed to accomplish relates to consecutive series without a loss, and puts to shame the feats of many of Test cricket's greatest teams. For those unfamiliar with the game, Test cricket is split into series which are typically three to five games long, and in the absence of anything grander to play for, winning these has historically been the solitary end goal of every

CRICKET TEAM: THE WEST INDIES, 1980S AND '90S

match. Some great teams have enjoyed extended periods without a series loss – the aforementioned Aussies either won or drew 16 consecutive series, a streak which lasted close to four years. England nearly lasted the entire 1950s without a series loss, managing 14 in a row, while South Africa also enjoyed 14 successive series without defeat between 2009 and 2014.

The West Indies team of the '80s and '90s went unbeaten in 29 consecutive series, nearly twice as many as any other side in history. It started in 1980, when they beat England 1-0 in a five-game series. MTV was launched, Chernobyl exploded, the Berlin Wall came down and we began to near the new millennium before finally, in 1995, they handed the baton over to a burgeoning Australian team that beat them 2-1 in a series dominated by bowlers.

Over the course of 15 years, not a single team managed to beat them in a series. A number went close – of the 29 unbeaten series in a row, nine were drawn, but that was as near as anyone got.

The below graph highlights every instance in Test history in which a team managed to play at least ten consecutive series without losing any of them, something which happened on 14 occasions in the 145 years between the first ever Test match in 1877 and 2022. The length of each box within the graph represents the period of time during which the streak occurred, while the numbers refer to how many series were involved in the streak.

Of course, as the graph suggests there have been significant changes in the number of Tests played per year over the course of time, and as a result there are a few discrepancies. One Australian team, which would ultimately come to be aptly known as The Invincibles, went nearly two decades without a series loss, though a whole lot of global turmoil combined with the fact that they had to take a boat for many weeks to play a single series meant that they only accumulated 12 of them in that time. In contrast, the aforementioned

CRICKET TEAM: THE WEST INDIES, 1980S AND '90S

Australians of my childhood sit in second place of all-time in terms of consecutive series without a loss at 16, but that run lasted less than four years. Still, it's an interesting graph to highlight the West Indies' dominance both in terms of consecutive unbeaten series and the length of time for which this streak lasted, and the fact that they were able to maintain their position atop world cricket for such an extended period of time is a feat in itself.

Unsurprisingly given these gaudy numbers, theirs was a side littered with talent. Viv Richards' illustrious career saw him pound opposing bowling attacks from pillar to post as he etched his name into the history books as one of the game's greatest, and when he pulled up stumps in 1991 he handed the baton over to Brian Lara, whose reputation would ultimately go on to rival Viv's own. Clive Lloyd led the team into their period of dominance both as captain and an imposing middle-order batter, while Gordon Greenidge and Desmond Haynes combined for arguably the greatest opening partnership in the history of Test cricket history. Throw in Richie Richardson for good measure and you've got a team that could seriously wield the willow.

Any side boasting as many talented batters as this would be bound for plenty of success. And yet, in the history books they play second fiddle to what was a fearsome bowling attack. For all of their batting talent, the West Indies' incredible record and the aura of inexorability which they carried around with them were largely a product of their fast bowlers.

A look at the best bowling averages in Test cricket history paints a startling picture of just how good they were. Counting only players who began their career within the last century and played at least 25 matches – necessary not only to make my point, but also to weed out a whole lot of bowlers who played 20-odd matches in the late

1800s and early 1900s when stats were incomparable to today – Malcolm Marshall, Joel Garner and Curtly Ambrose fill positions 3-5 respectively, while Colin Croft sits at 24, Michael Holding is at 28, Ian Bishop is at 34 and Courtney Walsh is at 36. That's seven of the top 36 bowlers (and three of the top five) in 100 years of cricket history, all of whom averaged at or below 24.44. These bowlers are highlighted on the below graph in red. Incidentally, another West Indian of that era, Andy Roberts, sat not too far below them with an average of 25.61.

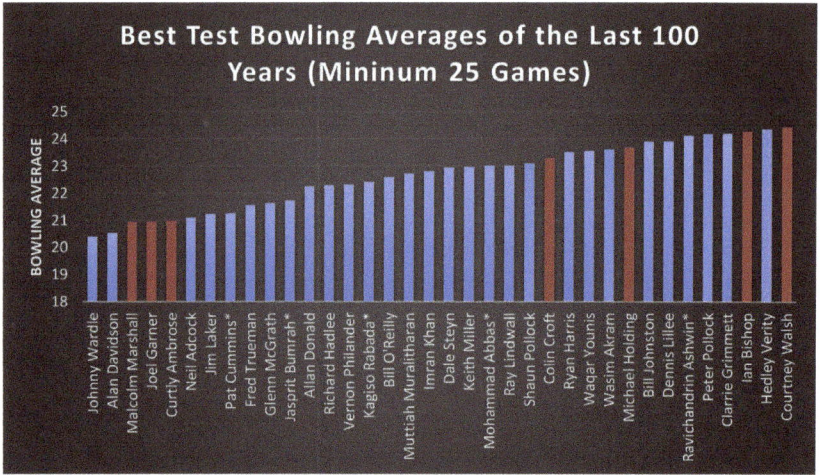

And they were fast. Though it's true that technology hadn't advanced to the point where their speeds were actually recorded on a consistent basis, the memories of fans who watched them and players who faced them, as well as footage which shows some of the best batters in the world facing them as though they had never before stepped on a cricket pitch, is all the proof we need.

The early signs of this team's impending period of dominance came in the late '70s, with a defining moment being when Pakistan visited in early 1977. Holding and Roberts already formed the basis of an intimidating attack, but when they were joined by debutants Garner and Croft, a quartet the likes of which Test cricket had never seen was born. Since dubbed The Four Horsemen of Death, these guys were as fast as it gets, and with four of them in the one side there was no respite for batters.

As physically imposing as they were fast, Roberts was the smallest of them at 6'2", or 188cm. Garner stood at 6'8". And they were mean. Garner was nicknamed Big Bird, and that was as friendly as their monikers got – Roberts became known as Hit Man, Croft was the Smiling Assassin, and perhaps scariest of all, Holding was referred to as the Whispering Death.

The latter tells the story of how his nickname came about like this: "The umpire couldn't hear me coming, he had to keep looking behind him to see if I was running in – and I suppose 'death' came from the pace at which I bowled – it could create death". His explanation is accompanied by a deadpan expression which belies the words coming out of his mouth, and concludes with an unassuming smile more appropriate for a waiter at an upmarket restaurant telling a diner to enjoy their meal than a 60-year-old man talking about killing people with a cricket ball.

Andy Roberts puts on a face of mock confusion when talking about his own nickname. "People say I was the hit man – I didn't go out to hit people, it's just that a lot of people got hit."

And the Smiling Assassin, well he might have been the craziest of them all. Garner tells a story of when they asked Croft what he would do if his mother was at the other end batting. Croft replied, "If my mother was at the other end, she's the target". Who knows, maybe he just didn't have a great relationship with his mum, but more likely this is testament to the appetite for destruction both he and his partners in crime possessed.

A year after The Four Horsemen came together, Malcolm Marshall, perhaps the most talented of all the fast bowlers to come out of the Caribbean during this period, joined them, and over the coming years Courtney Walsh, Ian Bishop and of course Curtly Ambrose (all 6'5" plus) would forge out careers as brilliant as they were terrifying of their own. It was a relentless period for the rest of world cricket, and with every big, fast, talented and seemingly apathetic-towards-hurting-people debutant who came along they must have let out a collective sigh.

The below table shows every series the West Indies played during this incredible 15-year period, with series they won in blue, series they drew in grey, and series they lost in red (there's no red). Overall during this period, they won 59 of their 115 matches, drew 41 and lost just 15.

Year	Opponent	W-L (Matches)	Result
1980	England	1-0 (5)	W
1980/81	Pakistan	1-0 (4)	W
1980/81	England	2-0 (4)	W
1981/82	Australia	1-1 (3)	D
1982/83	India	2-0 (5)	W
1983/84	India	3-0 (6)	W
1983/84	Australia	3-0 (5)	W
1984	England	5-0 (5)	W
1984/85	Australia	3-1 (5)	W
1984/85	New Zealand	2-0 (4)	W
1985/86	England	5-0 (5)	W
1986/87	Pakistan	1-1 (3)	D

CRICKET TEAM: THE WEST INDIES, 1980S AND '90S

Year	Opponent	W-L (Matches)	Result
1986/87	New Zealand	1-1 (3)	D
1987/88	India	1-1 (4)	D
1987/88	Pakistan	1-1 (3)	D
1988	England	4-0 (5)	W
1988/89	Australia	3-1 (5)	W
1988/89	India	3-0 (4)	W
1989/90	England	2-1 (4)	W
1990/91	Pakistan	1-1 (3)	D
1990/91	Australia	2-1 (5)	W
1991	England	2-2 (5)	D
1991/92	South Africa	1-0 (1)	W
1992/93	Australia	2-1 (5)	W
1992/93	Pakistan	2-0 (3)	W
1993/94	Sri Lanka	0-0 (1)	D
1993/94	England	3-1 (5)	W
1994/95	India	1-1 (3)	D
1994/95	New Zealand	1-0 (2)	W

Of particular note is their record against England, who earned themselves the unenviable title of the bunnies of perhaps cricket's greatest ever team. Incredibly, the Windies managed to navigate the entire 1980s without losing a solitary game to the nation from which cricket originated, going 17-0 from 24 matches against them over the course of the decade. It is worth noting that the Poms weren't at their best in the '80s, but you can only beat the teams in front of you and a 17-0 record suggests that the West Indies did just that.

As you can see in the above table, the height of their dominance came in the first half of the '80s, during which they won 28 games, drew 21 and lost just two. This was when Malcolm Marshall, Joel Garner and Michael Holding were at the peak of their powers, rolling through opposition batting line-ups consisting of the world's best players like they were schoolchildren.

As they entered the second half of the decade, however, a previously absent sense of fallibility began to follow the ageing team. When they welcomed England for a five-match series at the beginning of 1986, many (predominantly English people) thought the visitors had a chance of ending the West Indies' dominance against them, and with it what was then an almost six-year unbeaten series streak.

The West Indies won 5-0. While those advocating England's chances were proven wrong over the course of that five-match drubbing, however, they were onto something – the previously untouchable West Indian side was beginning to waver, and it wouldn't be until two and a half years later when they visited England that they would win another series.

Throughout the rest of 1986, 1987 and the first half of 1988, the side went through something of a transition phase. Garner and Holding, both nearing their mid-30s, were past their best, and after they each missed the drawn series against Pakistan at the end of 1986, the duo wound up their careers early the next year against New Zealand – another drawn series. Fortunately, a young Courtney Walsh was there for them to hand the baton to, but a bowling attack led by him and Malcolm Marshall didn't yet pose the threat of the side from a few years prior.

They would spearhead the attack as the West Indies drew against India and then Pakistan once again over the next year, making it four consecutive 1-1 tied series. The world had enjoyed some form of respite from the most formidable team of all time, but unfortunately for the world, perhaps the scariest bowler of them all was only just getting his career underway.

In the middle of 1988, Curtly Ambrose joined Malcolm Marshall, then 30 years old, and a 25-year-old Courtney Walsh for the second series of his career as the West Indian cricket team headed across the Atlantic to try to regain their swagger of old against the team which had played such a key role in giving it to them – England. Though the past couple of years hadn't seen the dominance to which everyone had become so accustomed, they'd still managed to avoid losing a series, and the streak was by this stage at 15 – and nearing a decade old.

But if the world had breathed a sigh of relief at the prospect of an apparent end to their reign, they quickly sucked it back in as the Windies won 4-0. Marshall, Garner and Holding had annihilated anyone in their wake throughout the first half of the '80s, but in this series a new three-headed monster emerged – an ageing but still dominant Marshall, a continually developing Courtney Walsh, and the emerging Curtly Ambrose. Marshall was still the leader – he had an extraordinary series, picking up 35 wickets at an average of just 12.65 – but Ambrose slotted in as a terrifying second fiddle, grabbing 22 wickets – well ahead of the third best-performed bowler of the series – at 20.22 and re-igniting the fear that had dwindled in the prior couple of years.

Those three helped to re-establish the West Indies as the world's best team over the next few years, and by the time Marshall retired in 1991, they had enjoyed 22 consecutive unbeaten series. Ambrose and Walsh continued on as the face of the bowling attack thereafter, and with Ian Bishop having joined them in hurtling bullets down the pitch in 1989, were able to continue the streak until 1995.

But when twin brothers Mark and Steve Waugh put on a 231-run partnership to help Australia to a thumping victory in the fourth Test of their 1995 series against the West Indies, it gave them a 2-1 series win and finally, after 15 long years, brought an end to the men from the Caribbean's unbeaten series streak.

For the rest of the '90s they remained a decent team, albeit far from the force they once were, but a couple of decades in the 21st century hasn't been kind to them. Continued issues both on and off the field have plagued them, and a growing desire on the part of their players to commit to the shorter, more lucrative 20-over form of the game has seen the Test side become borderline uncompetitive. In fact, in the 15 years between the beginning of 2007 and the end of 2021, their series record stood at 11 wins, eight draws and 30 losses (11-8-30), a far cry from the 20-9-0 they managed between 1980 and 1995.

No longer do they pump out fast, intimidating and talented fast bowlers as though they were created in a factory. Batters like Brian Lara and Viv Richards are nostalgic memories of a bygone era, and today they more closely resemble the struggling English side which they so enjoyed beating up on in the '80s – and that's being generous.

Comparing them to the West Indies of the late 20th century, of course, is unfair – it was perhaps the most dominant side in cricket history, and going unbeaten in 29 consecutive series is a feat which will likely never be matched. Certainly the 15 years without a series loss seems out of reach – even the West Indies, who play less Test cricket these days than many other sides, played 20 more series in the aforementioned 15 years than they did between 1980 and 1995, so for a team to sustain a streak for that long would likely need to stave off defeat for in excess of 50 series.

Significant periods of the 1980s and '90s also saw a distinct lack of any other great teams. The English, as mentioned on one or two or ten occasions, weren't much chop, and the Aussies too were going through a difficult period. South Africa was too busy with issues slightly more significant than cricket like Apartheid to bother fielding a team until 1992, India rarely won during the entirety of the '80s, and Sri Lanka was only a newbie to the international cricket circuit. New Zealand was one team that was consistently competitive, but though the West Indies' record may have benefited from the fact that the two sides didn't play very often, the men from the Caribbean did still win four and lose just one of the nine matches they played against one another during the streak. The biggest challenger to the West Indies during the era was probably Pakistan, so it's no surprise that the Windies didn't quite enjoy the dominance against Imran Khan and co as they did against England, though a record of six wins, seven draws and three losses between 1980 and 1995 suggests they still had the upper hand.

But ask anyone who had the pleasure of watching, or the misfortune of playing, the West Indies during the era, and they'll tell you that this side didn't need meek opposition to flex their collective muscle. They churned out fast bowlers like no other side in history ever has nor likely will, and had their fair share of brilliant batters to go with it. The fear generated by the likes of Ambrose, Marshall, Walsh and Garner is firmly embedded in cricket folklore, and certainly not only because of a lack of quality opposition. Somehow, the team managed to produce a large proportion of the greatest fast bowlers the world has ever seen within a decade, and with numerous generational batters thrown into the mix, a 15-year period of dominance was the result – a period which far surpasses that which any other team has managed before, and likely ever will.

By the Numbers

- The West Indies **won or drew 29 consecutive series** during a streak which lasted for **15 years**. The **next longest streak of consecutive unbeaten series is 16**, a number which Australia managed early this century.

- During this time, the West Indies **won 20 series and drew 9**.

- They **lost just 15 matches** in this 15-year period, while **winning 59 and drawing 41**.

- Their lethal fast bowling attack included **3 of the top 5 bowlers in history** by average, as well as **7 of the top 36**.

4

Tennis Event: John Isner vs Nicolas Mahut

I OFTEN WONDER what tennis would be like if the scoring system was different. Don't get me wrong, I'm a fan of the sport, but sometimes I think it would be far less interesting if the winner was just determined by the first player to win 50 points, for example, rather than the fairly arbitrary system which is actually employed. Fortunately for this book that's not the case, and the way the sport is scored leaves open the possibilities for some extremely anomalous score lines.

It was around dinner time on Tuesday, 22 June 2010 when John Isner and Nicolas Mahut stepped out onto Court 18 for their first round Wimbledon clash. The match didn't present as one which would draw significant interest – the American Isner was the 23rd seed, while Frenchman Mahut had been forced to battle his way through the qualifying rounds just to earn his place in the tournament.

Mahut, however, defied the odds over the course of that evening. After dropping the first set he won the next two, and when Isner responded with a victory in the fourth, the already lengthy match was called off for the evening, three hours after it first began. No one could have predicted what was to come, but the fact that there had been just two breaks of serve throughout the match and none in the third or fourth sets certainly gave the indication that neither player would be able to wrap things up particularly quickly when they came back on Wednesday.

And they didn't. The next day they resumed at 2:05pm – seven hours later, the match was still going, the light was again fading, and proceedings were brought to a halt for the second day in a row, this time with scores locked at 59 apiece in the fifth set. Isner's feet were bleeding, Mahut couldn't see properly, and the match wasn't yet finished.

Both returned on Thursday on fairly minimal sleep (why they couldn't sleep after playing seven hours of tennis is beyond me) and fortunately had to play for just a little over an hour before Isner took out the match 6-4, 3-6, 6-7, 7-6, 70-68. I remember watching a match at the 2003 Australian Open when I was ten years old in which Andy Roddick beat Younes El Aynaoui 21-19 in the fifth set, and I thought it was the craziest thing I'd ever seen. Little did I know it would fall almost 100 games short of a match played seven years later.

In all the Isner-Mahut marathon lasted for 11 hours and five minutes, and included a final set of eight hours and 11 minutes. There were 183 games played in total, and unsurprisingly it broke all sorts of records. At 47-47 in the final set, the scoreboard stopped functioning as it was only programmed to go to 47. Why 47? You'd have to ask IBM, but I'd fathom a guess that they never anticipated it would be relevant. The online scoreboard managed to make it to 50 and for the 38 games which remained – a number which would be enough

TENNIS EVENT: JOHN ISNER VS NICOLAS MAHUT

on its own to comprise a pretty lengthy match – users were told to add 50 to the score which was showing on the screen.

Presumably, both players wanted to go home and sleep for a week following the match, but unfortunately they each still had more tennis to play. Isner, of course, had a second round match to suit up for. In a peculiar quirk of fixturing he was drawn against another player who had endured a long five-setter in the first round in Thiemo de Bakker; he had won that match 16-14 in the fifth set. De Bakker wouldn't have expected to be heading into his second round clash with a distinct fitness advantage following his arduous first round win, but he was gifted a giant American with severely depleted energy sources and disposed of the more highly rated Isner in just 74 minutes. Isner was also scheduled to play doubles, but he and partner Sam Querry made what was probably a wise move and withdrew.

Mahut also had a doubles match to play and, incredibly, began it in the evening of the same day that his match with Isner concluded, and on the very same court – a court he probably never wanted to see again. That match also ended up being spread over three days, but fortunately for Mahut he spent most of that time waiting for his partner's singles match to finish; his doubles clash ended in four relatively normal length sets.

Clearly this was no ordinary tennis match, but just how much of a statistical outlier was it? As it turns out, a pretty big one, no matter which way you look at it.

The second longest match in professional history in terms of time was a doubles match played at the 2013 Davis Cup, in which the Czech Republic's Tomáš Berdych and Lukáš Rosol spent seven hours and one minute battling it out against Switzerland's Stanislas

Wawrinka and Marco Chiudenelli. The Czechs got the chocolates in that one, winning in five tight sets 6-4, 5-7, 6-4, 6-7, 24-22. Of course, while that is some sort of match, Isner and Mahut were forced to endure the added difficulty of having to cover the entire court by themselves, rather than sharing that duty with a partner.

The next longest – and the second longest singles match in history – was played between Leonardo Mayer and João Silva at the 2015 Davis Cup, and that lasted for six hours and 43 minutes – still almost an hour and a half shorter than the final set alone of the Isner-Mahut epic, and roughly four hours and 22 minutes less than the match in total. In other words, you could have played the second longest singles match ever 1.65 times before it would rival the longest.

The graph below depicts the 25 longest singles matches in professional tennis history, beginning with Isner-Mahut at the top. I've removed doubles matches for the aforementioned reason that to an extent players split their athletic duties when playing with a partner, as well as the fact that, to be completely frank, I just can't find all the records for the longest doubles matches. The graph wouldn't change significantly regardless, so I've just stuck with singles.

Even in a list of the longest matches ever, number one stands out like a sore thumb. In a graph which wasn't limited purely to the longest matches, and instead included every professional match in history, presumably the largest cluster would come around the two-three hour mark, and all the matches on the below graph would be very much on the outside edge of the plotted data. The Isner-Mahut match would appear even further out there on its own than it is below. Unfortunately plotting the length of every single professional tennis match in history would be a little too time-consuming, so we'll just have to make do with the top 25.

TENNIS EVENT: JOHN ISNER VS NICOLAS MAHUT

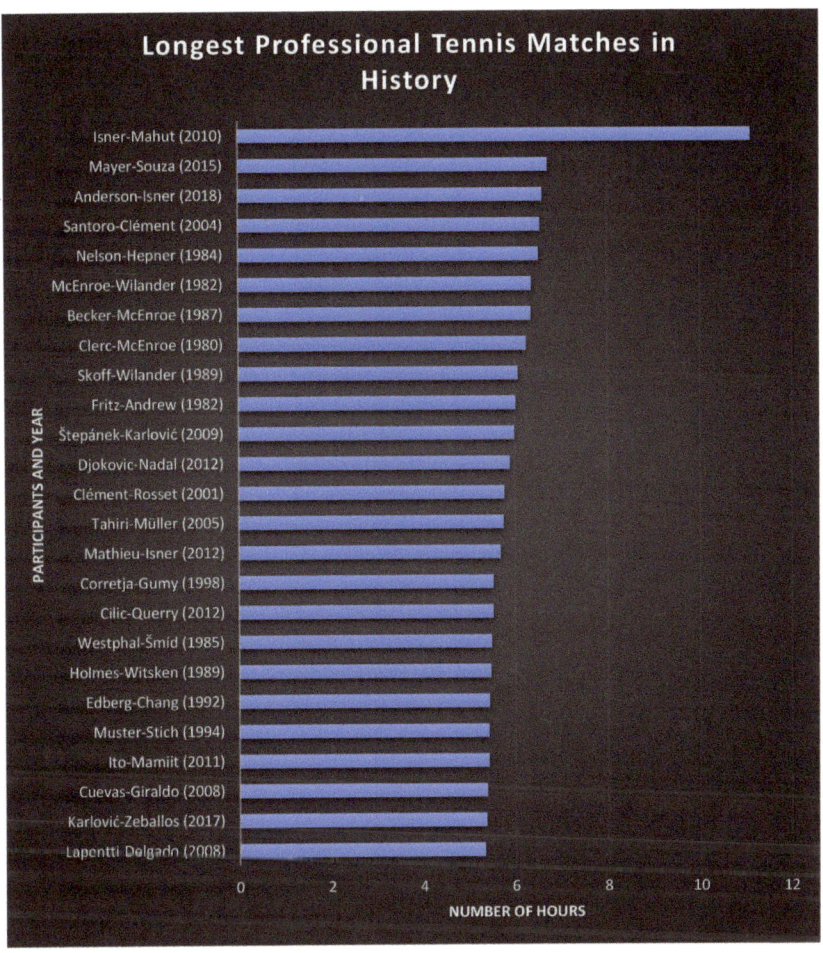

A side note: almost certainly the second most interesting match on the above graph is that of Nelson and Hepner (1984). The only women's match to feature, it lasted for over six and a half hours despite the fact that it only involved two sets. I genuinely thought there was an error when I first read that but there isn't, so while it isn't overly anomalous in any quantifiable way I've included a short chapter about it following this one.

Back to Isner and Mahut – in terms of total games, this match is equally unusual. A 1973 Davis Cup doubles match between

America's Stan Smith and Erik van Dillen, and Chile's Patricio Cornejo and Jaime Fillol, had the second most games – 122 in total courtesy largely of a 39-37 second set. Of course, Isner and Mahut played 16 more games than that in the fifth set alone, and 61 more games in total. American compatriots Pancho Gonzales and Charlie Pasarell earned themselves the coveted prize of the second longest singles match in history in terms of games, having played out a 112-game thriller at Wimbledon back in 1969. 12th seed Gonzales won that one 22-24, 1-6, 16-14, 6-3, 11-9.

Funnily enough, this outlier gets even stranger. For those unfamiliar with the scoring system in tennis, at the time of the Isner-Mahut marathon all sets except for the last went to a tiebreak if the scores reached 6-6, with the winner of that the winner of the set. Prior to the 1970s, however, tiebreaks weren't widely used at all, and sets continued until someone led by two games. This means that all five sets had the opportunity to drag on for an inordinate amount of time, not just the last.

You may have noticed that this was the case in the aforementioned Gonzales-Pasarell classic, in which three of the five sets had in excess of 20 games. In fact, six of the 25 matches on the graph above involved at least one of the first four sets extending past 6-6. It wasn't until 1989 that tiebreaks were introduced at the Davis Cup, and the six-hour, 22-minute slog between John McEnroe and Mats Wilander had in excess of 13 games (the maximum in a tiebreak set) in three of its five sets. Five years later, again at the Davis Cup, McEnroe played a match which lasted just one minute less against Boris Becker courtesy of a 15-13 second set and an 8-10 third, while in 1980 McEnroe was involved in ANOTHER match in excess of six hours which had only four sets. Fortunately, Isner and Mahut weren't subjected to this – considering that both the third and the fourth set went to tiebreaks, and the only set which couldn't lasted longer than any other entire singles match in history, they might still be playing today if tiebreaks didn't exist.

Though there's no single reason to explain how one match could be so much longer than any other, the serving ability of both Isner and Mahut can at least help. Of course, there have been plenty of meetings between good servers in history and typically they don't see 168 consecutive held service games, but this match was destined to see very few service breaks and at least a couple of tiebreaks. Indeed, Isner is a serial offender, having also been involved in the third longest singles match in history at six hours and 36 minutes against fellow big-server Kevin Anderson at Wimbledon in 2018. The 6'10" American must have had an eerie sense of déjà vu during that one, but fortunately for the sake of his own sanity he was beaten 26-24 in the last.

That Isner-Anderson match was ultimately the catalyst for both Wimbledon and the Australian Open to follow the US Open and introduce tiebreaks in the final set, removing the possibility of the never-ending matches which Isner seems so fond of. Roland Garros resisted for a few years, but in 2022 they were forced to join the tiebreak party too.

Which means, of course, that the already slim chances of this record ever being broken are now virtually next to none. Given the introduction of tiebreaks in all but the final set throughout the latter stages of the 20th century, it was probable even prior to this match that the majority of history's longest matches would have already taken place. Isner and Mahut along with a handful of others have bucked the trend, but it seems that for the most part, the days of matches lasting in excess of six hours plus is nearly over. Isner, Mahut and their bleeding feet wrote their name in the history books in 2010, and it's highly unlikely they'll ever be removed.

By the numbers

- At **11 hours and 5 minutes**, the match was **4 hours and 4 minutes longer** than any other in history, and **4 hours and 22 minutes longer** than any other singles match.

- The final set lasted **8 hours and 11 minutes**, more than an hour longer than any other professional match in history.

- The **183 games** played were **61 more than any other match** in professional tennis history and **71 more than any other singles match**.

- The **138 games in the final set** were still comfortably more than any other match in its entirety.

- **168 service games** were held in succession.

- Mahut won **502 points** compared to **Isner's 478**.

- Isner served **113 aces** and Mahut **served 103**. The previous most by a single player in a match was 78.

- Mahut won service games to stay in the match **63 times**.

- There were **3 breaks of serve** in the entire match.

5

Tennis Event: Vicki Nelson v Jean Hepner

THIS MATCH PIQUED my interest while researching the Isner-Mahut clash. It stands alone as relatively comfortably the longest women's match in professional tennis history at almost an hour and a half longer than any other, and yet, unlike literally every other match in the top 167 (as far back as I can find records for), it required only two sets. Theoretically Nelson won it pretty easily.

The final score was 6-4, 7-6 – a scoreline which would probably normally require around 1.5 hours to get through. This one took six hours and 31 minutes. So why did it take so long?

One explanation is the 643-shot, 29-minute-long rally which took place during the second set tiebreak. Unsurprisingly that's the longest point in pro tennis history, and is longer than numerous recorded matches.

The 13-11 tiebreak alone went for an hour and 47 minutes, meaning that even excluding that rally, it took an hour and 18 minutes to play 23 points – or an average of around 3.39 minutes per point. Obviously they were very evenly matched, and you would hope that they were also extremely slow between points.

Having taken place in the mid '80s at a fairly minor tournament, there's not a whole lot of recorded information about it, but I think it would be relatively safe to say that this is the match with the longest average game in tennis history. With just 23 games taking place over the course of six and a half hours, they were getting through less than four per hour – or roughly one every 17 minutes. For comparison, Isner and Mahut were getting through one game every 3.63 minutes.

Funnily enough it was a relatively inconsequential match – a first rounder at the Virginia Slims Ginny of Richmond tournament. Nelson would go on to lose in the second round. It was also played between two women who never reached great heights in the sport. Hepner's Wikipedia page begins, 'Jean Hepner is a former professional tennis player from the United States'. It then goes on to describe the match against Nelson, and that's pretty much it.

Nelson doesn't get a whole lot more. Her Wikipedia page begins, 'Vicki Nelson-Dunbar is a former professional tennis player from the United States. During her career she won one top-level singles title (at São Paulo in 1986), and reached the fourth round of the US Open in 1982.' Her match against Hepner is then described, and thus the page concludes.

For all intents and purposes it was a match of very little importance. And yet, almost four decades later, it remains one of the most unusual in the sport's history.

6

Swimming Career: Michael Phelps

An entire pizza and close to half a kilogram of pasta. It's enough to feed a small family, but for a 23-year-old Michael Phelps it was a pretty typical dinner. According to most sources you'll read, it would be followed by 1,000 calories of energy drinks and preceded by another 450 grams of pasta, roughly five big fat sandwiches, five eggs, a bunch of French toast and pancakes and a big bowl of porridge. There were also a few other bits and pieces thrown in there to make up the daily diet of the most successful Olympian of all time. All in all, Phelps was consuming around 12,000 calories per day – or so it's said.

Back in 2017, however, Phelps made a shock admission – the legendary 12,000 calorie-per-day diet was a myth! Speaking at an event in New York City, Phelps attempted to clear up all the hoo-ha surrounding his diet, because, according to him, some of the stories about how much he ate were 'ridiculous'. Rather than eating 12,000 calories per day like a bear loading up for hibernation, the reality was he only ate between 8,000 and 10,000 calories at his peak…maybe something like a bear on a normal day.

Regardless, it seems like an unreasonable amount for one man to consume, and that's probably because it is. The reality is, however, that the incredible rate at which Phelps ate is testament to the dedication he had to his craft. After all, if you're consuming that much and still boasting the physique of a Viking, you must be doing a whole lot of exercise.

While he was eating around 8,000 or 10,000 or 12,000 or however many calories per day – somewhere between four and six times the typical amount for a man of his age – Phelps was training for the 2008 Beijing Olympics. And I guess it must have worked, because he went on to win the gold medal in all eight of the events in which he participated – incidentally, just one less than anyone else had won in their entire Olympic career as of 2022.

In total, Phelps won 23 golds over the course of his decorated career – 14 more than Larisa Latynina from the Soviet Union, Paavo Nurmi from Finland, and America's Mark Spitz and Carl Lewis, all of whom share second place in the all-time list with nine at the time of writing. This means that he won more than 2.5 times that of his nearest rival – anomalous to say the least.

But Phelps wasn't always destined for a career as one of the greatest athletes of all time. In fact, as a young kid, the dedication and focus which so defined him as an adult were notably absent. The young Phelps had significant difficulties focusing on a single thing at any one time – he would later be diagnosed with ADHD – and had seemingly endless reserves of energy. The first of these things probably didn't bode well for his potential as an elite athlete, but the second certainly did, and once he discovered swimming he would spend an inordinate amount of time using that energy in the pool – at times swimming for up to three hours after school.

SWIMMING CAREER: MICHAEL PHELPS

He would go on to participate in his first Olympic Games when he was just 15. He made the final and finished fifth in the 200-metre butterfly – an event most 15-year-olds would be happy to be able to even complete 10% of – but, for the first and only time, he didn't win a medal. At the next Olympics, in 2004, he won six gold medals and two bronze, at the one after that he won eight golds, in 2012 he managed a comparatively measly four golds and two silvers, and in his last hoorah in 2016 he went home with five golds and a silver.

The graph below demonstrates his performance at each Olympics in terms of gold medals (the blue), as well as his cumulative tally at that point in his career (the blue plus the red). The horizontal white line represents the careers of the aforementioned Larisa Latynina and co, the long-time equal second most successful Olympians of all time. As you can see, he went close to matching their career tallies in 2008 alone, was well past them in total golds by the end of the second Olympics at which he won medals, and by the end of his career they were just a speck in the rear-view mirror.

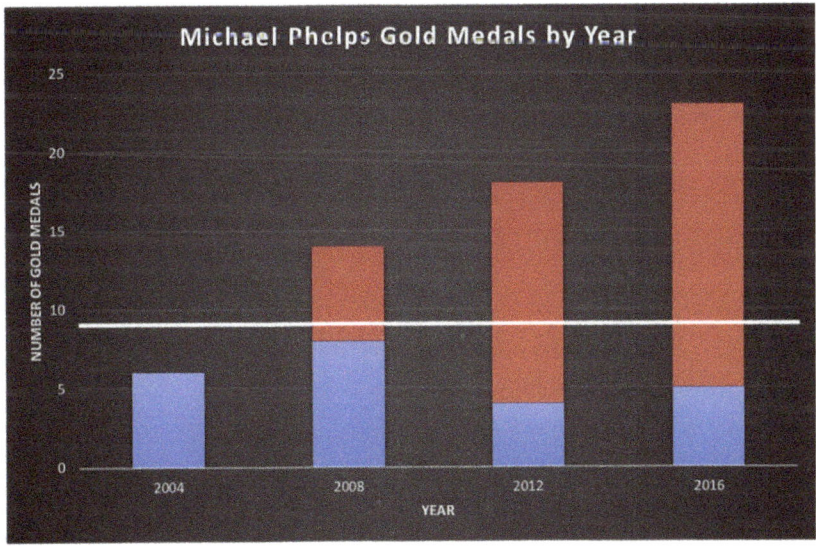

SPORT'S GREATEST STATISTICAL ANOMALIES

They're some pretty dominant numbers, and on those alone Phelps' career might be the biggest statistical outlier in sporting history – a career with more than 2.5 times more success than anybody else is pretty unheard of. And if the above isn't enough to demonstrate just how significantly he has outperformed literally every other Olympian in history, the below graph should help. It shows how many Olympians (at both the winter and summer games) have managed to win five Olympic golds, six Olympic golds and so on, all the way through to Phelps with 23.

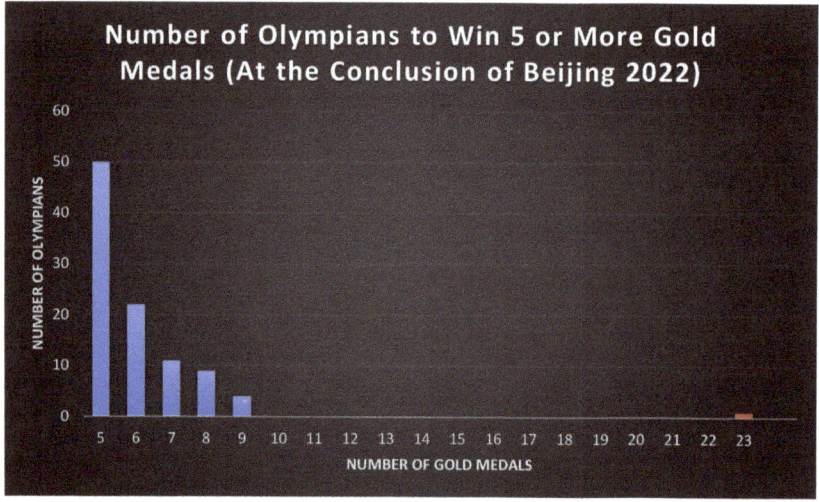

As you can see, Phelps' achievement is looking pretty lonely out there on 23. Next to him is a whole lot of empty space, before we finally see another line emerge at nine gold medals, a number which four athletes have reached to date. Working backwards from there the graph grows pretty exponentially, with 49 athletes having managed five, 130 at four and so on. The graph had to stop at five gold medals, however, because had it continued the y-axis would have grown to the point that Phelps' one-man tower would have been virtually invisible without the help of a microscope.

There's no doubting Phelps' credentials as a statistical outlier, but there are certain problems which arise with comparing athletes by gold medals at the Olympics because they don't all have the capacity to win the same number. Many athletes compete in just one event, while those in disciplines with multiple events often compete in two or three. Entering eight events at one Olympics obviously gives a competitor a greater chance of winning, well, eight gold medals – though it is still pretty unlikely.

But while he may not be 2.5 times better than any other Olympian in history, the numbers still speak to his dominance, and the caveat mentioned above doesn't take into account the fact that presumably it's harder to compete in eight events than one. While he may have entered into more races than virtually every other Olympian, there is something to be said for competing in up to eight different events across a handful of days, particularly given that many other competitors would have had their attention focused solely on one or two. Where Phelps had to train for numerous strokes and prepare for something close to peak performance often multiple times a day and up to 20 times at a given Olympics, others had the advantage of focusing all their attention on one or two events.

There are also plenty of other swimmers who have plied their trade across numerous different strokes, and none of them have gone close to reaching the lofty heights of Phelps. Perhaps the closest swimmer in history to matching him is the aforementioned Mark Spitz, who in just two Olympics in 1968 and 1972 managed nine gold medals, a silver and a bronze. Extrapolating that out to the four Olympics in which Phelps competed, Spitz would have won 18 golds and a total of 22 medals – closer than anyone else in history, but still just a little over 75% of Phelps' achievement, and it of course doesn't factor in the longevity of Phelps. Indeed, Phelps' performance in 2016 was lauded for the fact that the five golds he won came at the ripe old age of 31 in a sport where competitors tend to peak in their early 20s.

In fact, according to a study conducted by French researchers Geoffroy Berthelot and Stephane Len in 2011, which was based on data related to the careers of over a thousand swimmers and track-and-field athletes, swimming is one sport where peak performance is typically reached much earlier than in others. While in athletics the peak of a career was found to occur at around 26 years of age, this study suggested that the average peak for swimmers was just 21. Of course, everyone is different and this doesn't mean that no one peaks later, but it stands in line with Phelps enjoying his most successful Olympic appearances at the ages of 19 and 23. That he was still so dominant at 31 is impressive in itself, and it's unlikely that those with shorter careers and similar achievements would have been able to sustain their performance for as long as Phelps.

There is one other caveat – ten of Phelps' 23 gold medals came in relays for the USA. Can we punish him for the fact that a large portion of his individual success came as part of a team for which he contributed only 25% of the swim? Maybe a little, and in a handful of those, a dominant USA team won by a large enough margin that even with the next best option taking the place of Phelps they probably would have won. But in even more, the race was close enough that Phelps' absence could feasibly have resulted in the gold medal going elsewhere, so we can't exactly call them a result of the exploits of his teammates.

And in any case, even on individual events alone he is strokes ahead of his nearest rival in total gold medals. His 13 individual wins has him comfortably ahead of fellow American Ray Ewry, who won eight individual golds between 1900 and 1908 in what was presumably a very different looking Olympic games, and while there are a few who could potentially close the gap on him at Paris in 2024, it looks likely that he'll hold onto a pretty significant margin for a while yet. On individual wins alone Phelps might not have outperformed every other Olympian in history by a factor of 2.5, but 1.62 times more individual medals than anyone else is still pretty good.

By any measure, it's almost impossible to argue against him as the greatest Olympian of all time, and indeed one of the most dominant athletes in his field (or should I say pool) that we've ever seen. If he competed as his own country, the 23 gold medals he won would have made him the 44th most successful nation in Olympic history following the Beijing 2022 Winter Olympics – well over 100 years after gold medals were first awarded – and many of the nations on a similar number to him are consistently competitive at the Games. Jamaica, for example, always prominent on the track, only managed to surpass him at the aforementioned Tokyo Games, while the extremely talented distance runners from Ethiopia had, by the same point in time, led their country to the same number of total golds as Phelps.

The 2020 Tokyo Olympics, which of course took place in 2021, marked the first time this millennium that an Olympics took place without Phelps. Not that it bothered him. After the Rio Olympics in 2016, Phelps slipped pretty comfortably into home life with his wife Nicole, three kids, 23 gold medals and millions and millions of dollars. According to a 2019 interview with the New York Times, a standard day post-retiring involved him waking up early and making breakfast for the kids. The article didn't specifically mention how many calories each of those kids consumed (probably a reasonable omission) but apparently the middle child Beckett 'is a machine, he'll eat anything'. Like father, like son.

SPORT'S GREATEST STATISTICAL ANOMALIES

By the Numbers

- Phelps won **23 gold medals** throughout his career, **14 more than any other Olympian**.

- His total gold medal tally is **more than 2.5 times greater** than anyone else in history.

- Phelps' 2008 tally of **8 gold medals** is just 1 less than anyone else has ever won in total.

7

Golf Career: Tiger Woods

TIGER WOODS IS a polarising figure. For most golf lovers, he is the pinnacle of golfing royalty, the most enjoyable person to watch swing a club since clubs have been swung, and a talent who, at the peak of his powers, was so much better than his peers that comparisons were rendered irrelevant. For others, he's that guy who slept with a bunch of people he shouldn't have, crashed his car outside his ex-wife's house and then got dropped by half his sponsors. Regardless of what he means to you, in his prime he enjoyed a reign – or two, more aptly – at the top of the world golf rankings the likes of which will probably never be seen again.

Becoming the number one ranked player in the world takes some serious work. In fact, from the beginning of the Official World Golf Rankings back in 1986 up until the time of writing in 2022, just 25 players have enjoyed the view from the top of the mountain. Some of those 25 spent barely enough time up there to get a full 360° view – Tom Lehman had just a solitary week as world number one,

Bernhard Langer had a couple more than that, while even the great Ernie Els could only manage nine.

Tiger's cumulative total as the number one player in the world is 683 weeks, or a little over 13 years. In second place is Australia's Greg Norman, The Shark, whose 331 weeks is just shy of half Tiger's total. Making Woods' feat even more anomalous is the fact that, had he never existed, this chapter would have been about Norman, because as of 2022, Dustin Johnson is in third place with just 135. Johnson turned 38 this year while fourth-placed Rory McIlroy (106 weeks) turned just 33, so each of them has time to add more weeks to the tally, but it's probably safe to assume that they won't get close to Norman, let alone Woods.

It's a pretty commanding old lead that Tiger has put up on his peers, and to highlight the gap between he and the rest I've put together the graph that you'll see below, which includes the ten players who have spent the longest time as the world's number one ranked male player. This shows as rudimentarily as possible the chasm between Tiger and Norman, and Norman and the rest of the field.

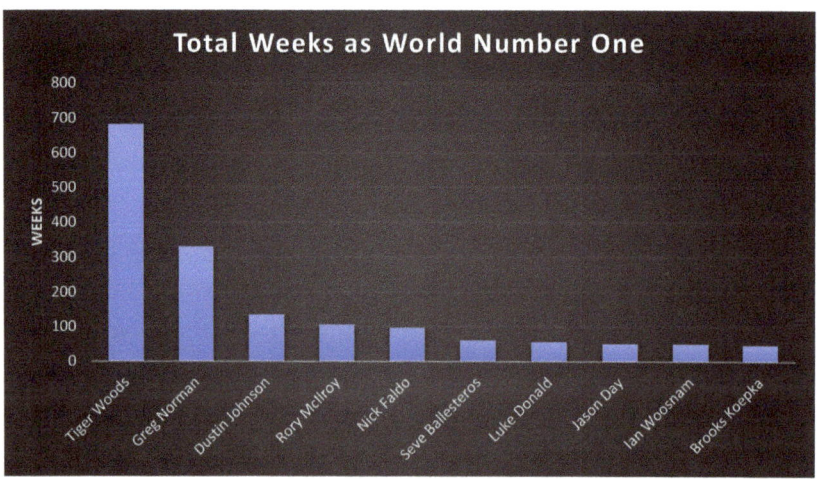

At the time of writing, you could stack up every player from Johnson through to Koepka and still have a significantly smaller tower (603) than what Woods has constructed. That could eventually change with a handful of the players from third through to tenth still playing at a high level, but fortunately this chapter has been completed in time to make reference to that statistic.

Prior to writing this chapter I was tossing up how to frame it, because Woods is also the owner of another related anomaly. As impressive as the above numbers are, they're arguably matched by the statistic of consecutive weeks as the world number one. Given Tiger has spent close to 40% of the time since the Official World Golf Rankings were introduced back in 1986 at the top of the table it's little surprise that he also boasts a significant lead over his rivals in consecutive weeks there, but the numbers are nonetheless fairly striking.

Tiger is in first with 281 successive weeks – or a little over five years – atop the rankings, a reign he enjoyed from 2005 until 2010. In second place is also Tiger, this time with 264 weeks, or again a little over five years. This period he enjoyed from 1999-2004. In third place is Greg Norman, who fell just short of 100 consecutive weeks as the number one ranked player in the world with 96, a little over one-third of Tiger's longest streak and a touch more than 36% of his second longest. The graph below shows the ten longest streaks as the world's number one player.

SPORT'S GREATEST STATISTICAL ANOMALIES

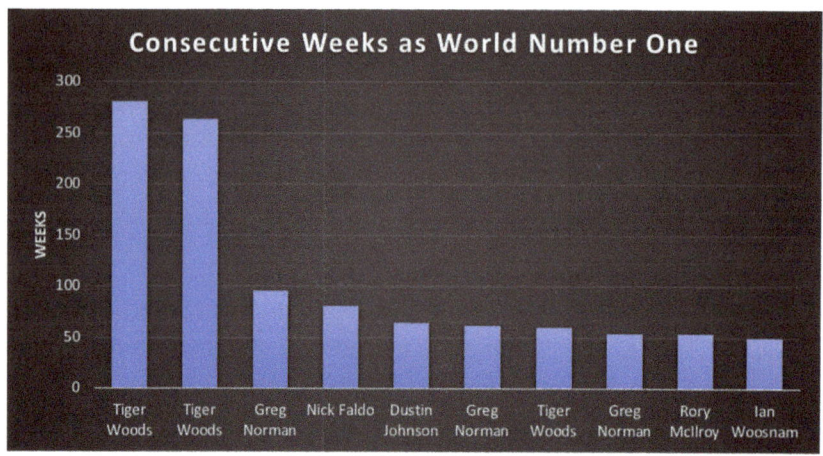

Clearly there's already a fairly hefty gap between Tiger and the rest in this stat, but making it even more extraordinary is just how close he came to joining these two streaks together to create one solitary streak – one which would have been more than five times longer than anyone else has ever managed. Between the 15th of August, 1999, and the 30th of October, 2010, just 32 weeks passed when Tiger wasn't the top ranked player in the world, all of which came in quick succession.

It was the 5th of September, 2004, when Fiji's Vijay Singh won the Deutsche Bank Championship in Boston by three strokes – Tiger finished in a tie for second – and famously stole the coveted position from the man who had owned it for so long. It was his sixth tournament win for the year, and he consolidated his place atop the world rankings by taking out the Canadian Open the very next week, before winning for a third time in the month of September two weeks later at the Pennsylvania Classic.

After those three wins the Fijian had opened up a sizeable lead over Tiger – who remained in second – and so would remain the world number one into the new year. But Tiger began working his way back throughout the early stages of 2005, and when he won the Duval Open in early March with a whopping -24 (Vijay was back in a tie for third at -19) he regained his seat on the throne. The two see-sawed back and forth for a couple of months, with Tiger winning The Masters in April and Vijay responding with two Tour victories in the month that followed, before Tiger broke away to begin the second of his five-year streaks.

Throughout the period during which Vijay was on top, Tiger was ranked second the entire time, aside from a couple of weeks when perennial rankings bridesmaid Ernie Els overtook him. But despite this, historically this period is recognised as a form slump during Tiger's era of dominance, even though he was usurped by a man having one of the greatest seasons in PGA Tour history. In that 2004 season which culminated with Vijay becoming the world's number one player, the Fijian accumulated the fifth most points in a calendar year since the rankings came into existence (points are accumulated based on your finish in a given tournament, with more points available for tournaments with stronger fields). So it wasn't as though Tiger was felled by some shmuck who happened to be in the right place at the right time – at the same time as he was a little off, Vijay was about as on as you can get. Incidentally, in the aforementioned list of most points in a calendar year on which Vijay's 2004 season sits fifth, Tiger owns positions 1, 2, 3, 4, 6, 7 and 9.

In what is something of a recurring theme in this book, Tiger responded to being knocked off his throne with vigour, putting together two of the best seasons of his glittering career in 2005 and 2006. After regaining the number one spot to begin what would ultimately be a 281-week stint there, he went on to win three tournaments – including The Open Championship – in the second half of the season to go with the three he had won earlier in the year. In 2006 he bettered this, winning a massive eight events, including five in just eight weeks during a stretch in which he won both The Open Championship (again) and the PGA Championship. Poor old Vijay didn't stand a chance.

To further understand his dominance, I thought it would be interesting to get some sense of how Tiger's years as number one compared to other players who spent time in the position. Was he just hanging onto a lead over the chasing pack during his 13 years at the top, or had he left his competitors so far in his dust that the prospect of a change atop the rankings wasn't even worth considering?

Unfortunately, there have been a number of changes to the way the rankings are calculated since they were created, so a direct comparison between points totals of various world number ones would throw up some erratic results. I decided instead to take a look at the lead the number one ranked players in the world have held over their number two counterparts over the years – after all, at least we can be certain that the world number one and the world number two at any given time were being ranked by the same scoring system. We know already that Tiger has spent an inordinate amount of time as the world number one, but this will give an indication of just how far ahead of the pack he was when he was there (or at least I hoped! Given how many hours this took it would have been disheartening if it didn't highlight his dominance).

Things begin to get a little statistically heavy here, but stick with me. The graph below is intended to highlight the gap between the number one and number two players in the world over time, but instead of being based on the points differential between these two players, it's based on the percentage difference between their rankings. Here's why: in the early stages of the Official World Golf Rankings, points were accumulated but not divided by total tournaments played, so while Tiger was spending time at number one with a ranking of 12 or 13 with opponents a point or so behind, 30 years ago players often had ranking totals in the thousands, with a gap of hundreds back to second. A graph using these numbers would make for pretty uninteresting viewing and would severely diminish Tiger's feats, thus the numbers have been standardised.

A score of 1.5 on the graph below, for example, would indicate that the world number one's ranking was 50% greater than that of the world number two – this could mean that his ranking was 15 and the world number two's was 10, or it could be 1,500 to 1,000. Of course, a graph with this statistic for every week since 1986 would be long enough to warrant an entire chapter in and of itself – and we've all got better things to do than spend hour after hour breaking down statistics for no good reason – so I've done the hard work for you. I broke it down into individual player streaks at world number one to better highlight player performance during specific time periods, and took the average weekly lead over the world number two for every occasion in which a player has been atop the rankings for at least 15 weeks.

I set the cut-off at 15 weeks partly because I was sick of all the number-crunching, but mostly because players who weren't world number one for an extended period don't have a chance to develop much of a lead over the man in pursuit. The ranking points change a relatively small amount week-to-week, so we can safely assume that the gap between the world number one and two was very minimal during streaks of less than 15 weeks (and most streaks of not much more than that, as you'll see below).

Aside from being one of the more arduous activities I've ever completed, this turned out to be a relatively illuminating way to demonstrate Tiger's supremacy over an extended period. Not only was he the best player in the world for far longer than anyone else in history (or more accurately, since 1986), but when he was the world's best player he was significantly further ahead of second place than other world number ones.

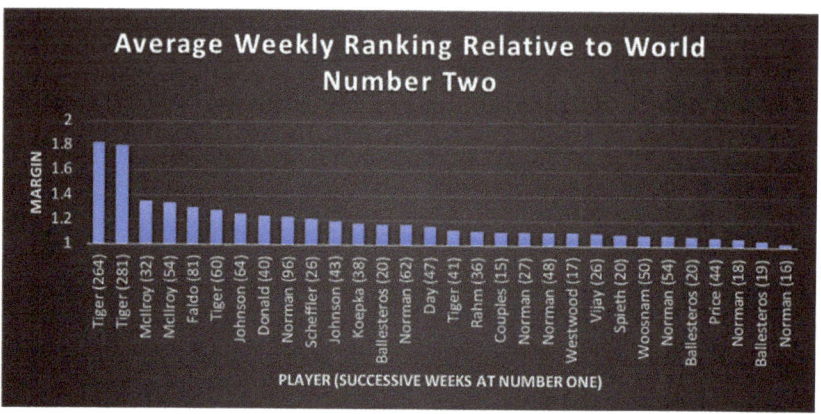

As you can see, Tiger's average weekly lead during both of his 5+ year streaks as world number one was over 1.8 (1.824 and 1.801, to be exact). Next is Rory McIlroy, who did well to average 1.35 times the ranking of his opponent in just 32 weeks, and aside from him again during his 54-week streak at the top and Nick Faldo during his 81 weeks there, no one else is close to 1.3. In fact, only nine times in history has a player had an average lead over the world number two of more than 1.2 during a streak at the top of the rankings – and three of those times it was Tiger.

Clearly there is a pretty hefty correlation between weeks at number one and how far ahead of number two you are, but still – in a rankings system which generally separates players by a fairly minimal amount, Tiger had on average nearly twice the ranking points of his nearest rival for over five years…twice.

GOLF CAREER: TIGER WOODS

The below graphs go into a little more detail about these two streaks, showing the week-to-week difference between Tiger and whoever happened to be the world number two at any given time. There was the occasional week missing in the archives, but regardless it gives a pretty comprehensive picture of how far ahead of his peers Tiger was for two extended periods.

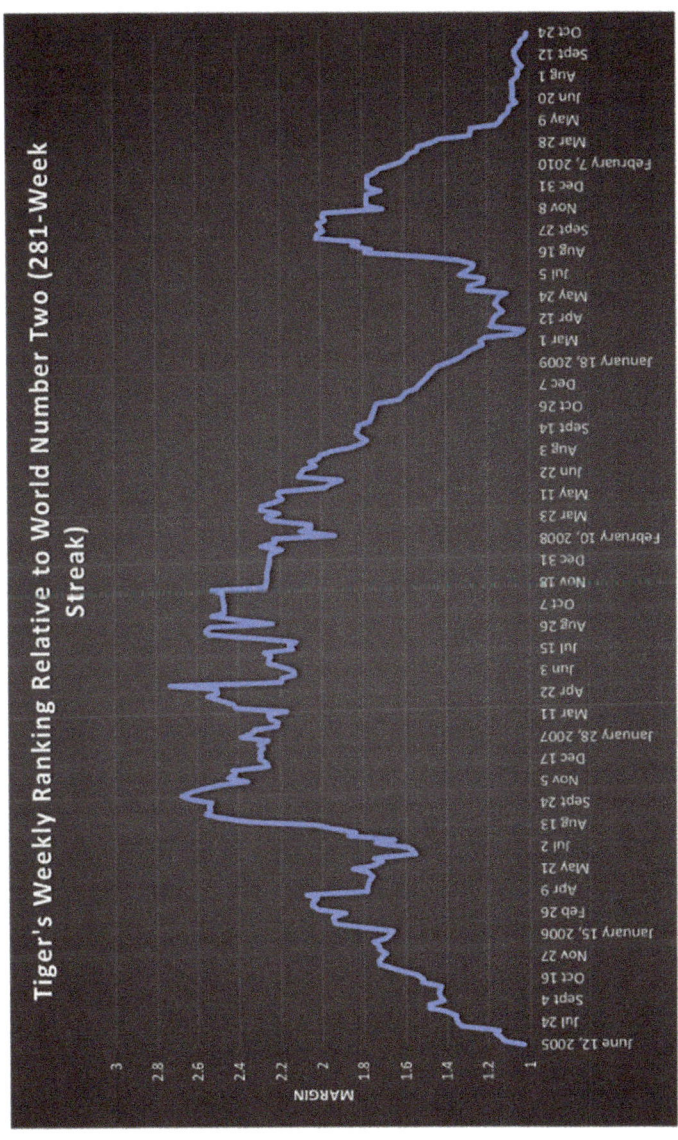

SPORT'S GREATEST STATISTICAL ANOMALIES

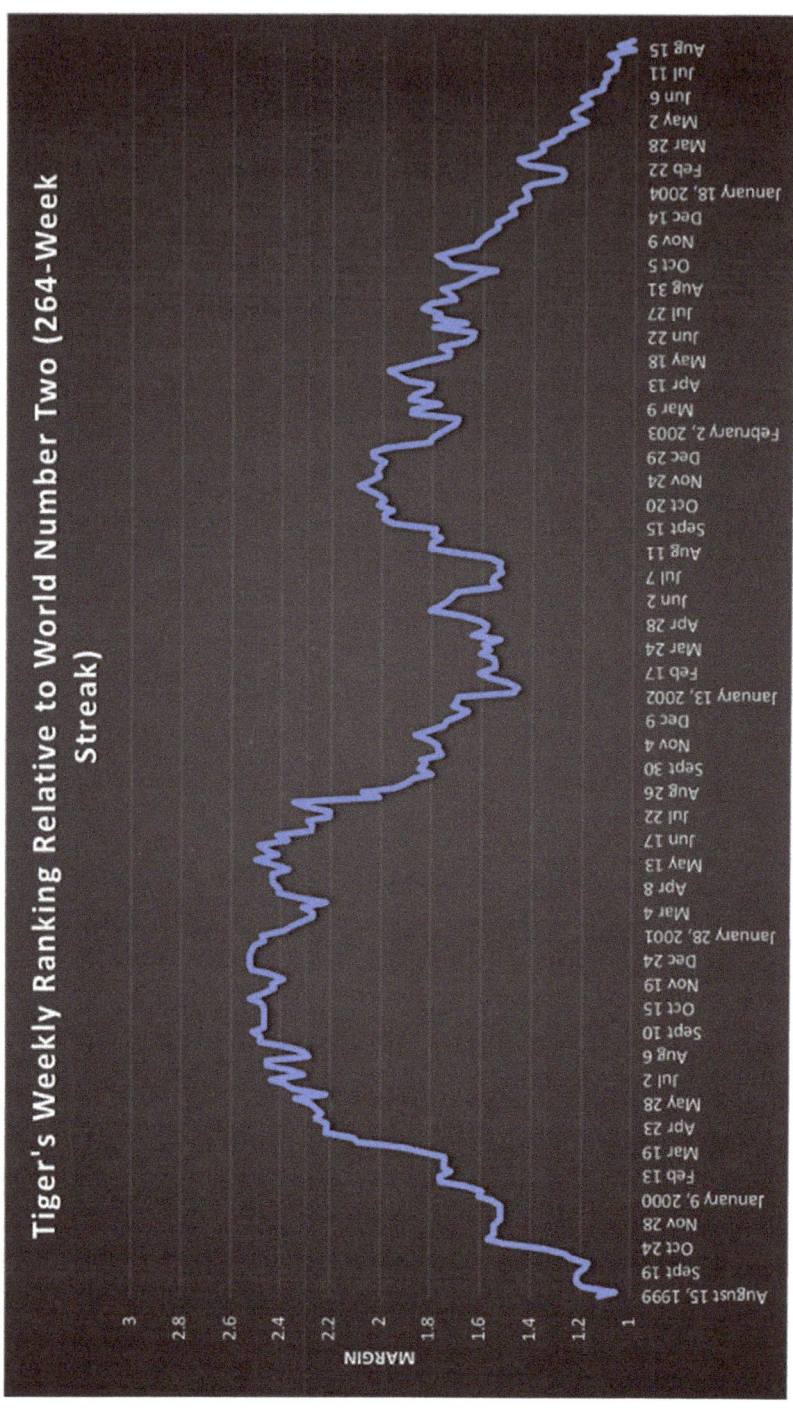

He maxed out on the 6th of May, 2007, at an incredible 2.73 times the ranking of the world number two (incidentally, his ranking on this date was 20.77, while Jim Furyk was in second – a position he became very much accustomed to – with 7.61). For reference, the biggest margin any player not named Tiger Woods has ever had over second place is 1.605 – that was Dustin Johnson back in mid-2017. During his longest streak, Tiger was above that mark for close to three successive years, as he was for the majority of his 264-week stint at the top.

These graphs also reveal a couple of other things of note, aside from just how peerless Tiger was during his extensive peak. In the first graph, which refers to the second and longest of his two enormous streaks, his lead shrunk rapidly during the second half of 2008 and early stages of 2009. This was no fault of his own – he incredibly won the 2008 US Open with a torn anterior cruciate ligament, which he had reconstructive surgery to repair after the tournament and missed eight months as a result. Subsequently, the lead of 2.11 which he held on the 15th of June, 2008, decreased pretty rapidly nearly every week until, on the 22nd of March the following year, it was just 1.02. Fortunately he had returned to the course a couple of weeks earlier, but having missed such an extended period of time his streak seemed almost certain to end at the hands of Phil Mickelson. Instead, Tiger went out and won the Arnold Palmer Invitational less than a month after his return, and would go on to win another five tournaments in the next six months to re-establish his lead.

Did he know that Phil was coming for him? Was Tiger motivated by his own streak and able to pull a rabbit out of the proverbial hat just as it appeared to be coming to an end? Did he watch his lead as world number one shrinking every week as he rehabbed his knee and wickedly machinate to return just in time to snatch it away from Mickelson's outstretched hand? You'd have to ask Tiger, but while one would assume there was some element of coincidence to it, it's also hard to imagine him not being aware of it, and as one of the most clutch sportspeople in history, perhaps the prospect of losing a grip on the world number one spot was a motivating factor.

During that period in which he won six events in six months to stave off Mickelson, Tiger managed to rebuild a ranking almost two times that of his nearest rival by the end of September. Soon after, however, his life off the course came tumbling down around him and his life on it was put on hold. It started with claims of extramarital relations, included a car crash near his home, and ended with him taking a few months off from the game beginning in late 2009. He would return in April of 2010, but when he did his appearances were only intermittent, and his form scratchy at best.

Still, he managed to eke out nearly a year of extra time as the world number one, despite barely taking to the course. His challengers squabbled away below him, and it must have been a point of significant frustration for players who had spent so much time competing for the number two position that it took so long for them to get past Tiger, even when he wasn't playing.

As his time at number one during the second streak began to near a close, it was as though a forcefield separated him from second place. Points dropped off his ranking by the week, but Mickelson, who must have felt like he had been the number two player in the world for half of his life, continued to lose points off his own, meaning the gap between first and second stayed much the same for months despite the fact that Tiger wasn't playing. And, when finally there was a change at the top, it wasn't Phil who took over – he had slipped behind Lee Westwood just a handful of weeks prior. The race for world number one which nobody appeared to want to win was as enthralling for fans as it must have been frustrating for the players involved. And, while it's purely a point for speculation, you would assume Tiger would have held onto the position for much longer had his personal life not come tumbling down around him.

But speculation is just that, and perhaps even without all the off-course tumult something else would have cursed him. The idea that his streak of 281 weeks at number one was cut short by off-course matters, however, is certainly worth thinking about, and one has to wonder how long that streak would have lasted had he not plagued himself with these issues. Regardless of the hypotheticals though, his time at the top of world golf was more than sufficient to claim one of the more impressive statistical anomalies in sporting history.

As always, however, there is a caveat. I don't like them, you don't like them, but with the exception of Don Bradman's career (which we'll look at in the next chapter) they always exist, and in this case it is how recently these rankings began to be calculated. There are numerous players widely considered to be in the conversation for the greatest golfer of all time whose careers took place prior to the publishing of these rankings in 1986, and there's every chance that one or more of them could have held a candle to Tiger's stretch at the top. In fact, before the start of the Official World Golf Rankings in 1986, unofficial end of year world golf rankings were developed by Mark McCormack in his annual *World of Professional Golf* publication from 1968 to 1985. McCormack's rankings listed Jack Nicklaus as the world number one from 1968 to 1977 – ten years in succession – and that could easily have been longer had they begun earlier given Nicklaus had already been dominant for years when they were first published. Tom Watson then led these rankings for five consecutive years between 1978 and 1982, before Seve Ballesteros enjoyed three years at the top.

All these streaks, of course, would rival if not better those of Tiger, but these rankings were only published once per annum, accumulating all the results over the course of that year. So while Nicklaus was, according to these rankings, the best player in the world for ten consecutive years, he wouldn't necessarily have been leading a weekly ranking system throughout the duration of that time period. Likewise for Watson and Ballesteros.

Greg Norman never finished on top of these season-long rankings, but he too would be justified in claiming that he deserves to be a little closer to Tiger in total weeks at number one than the 352 weeks which separates them. When the *Official* World Golf Rankings began, he was already 31 years of age, and had for a number of years been successful on the European Tour. It wasn't until 1983 that he joined the PGA Tour though, and it was in 1986, the first year that the official rankings were published, that he began to put a gap on his rivals. His best years certainly came once the rankings were official, but nonetheless he was there or thereabouts for a couple of years prior and may have squeezed out a few more weeks at number one had they been published earlier.

But as the old adage goes, if ifs and buts were candy and nuts we'd all have a merry Christmas. What that truly means who really knows, but I guess the point is that things are as they are. The rankings began in 1986, and since then Tiger has enjoyed a dominance both in length and in strength that is unparalleled by his peers. He had close to triple the ranking points of any rival for an extended period using a system in which no other player has ever developed a lead of more than around 60% over their opponents, has spent more than double the amount of time of any other player as world number one over the past 35 years, and closer to six times that of any other player aside from Greg Norman. Maybe Jack Nicklaus or Arnold Palmer or Gary Player or somebody else would have got closer had they had the opportunity, but fortunately for the purpose of this outlier, they never got the chance.

By the Numbers

- Woods has spent a total of **683 weeks as the world number one**. Greg Norman is **second with 331 weeks**, while Dustin Johnson is **third with 135.**

- Woods had separate streaks of **281 weeks and 264 weeks consecutively** as world number one; Greg Norman has the **third longest streak at 96 weeks.**

- During those two extended streaks, Woods' world ranking points were **on average more than 1.8 times** greater than the world number two; the **next highest average lead during a period as world number one by any player is 1.35.**

- The most significant lead Woods ever had as world number one came when he had **2.73 times more ranking points** than world number two Jim Furyk; the **biggest lead by any other player as world number one is 1.605.**

8

Cricket Career: Don Bradman

DON BRADMAN IS almost certainly the greatest statistical anomaly in the history of sport. He is to sporting outliers what Einstein is to physics; what Shakespeare is to literature. In a field of sporting GOATs, he stands alone as the best of them. He is the GOAT of the GOATs. That's not to disparage the exploits of the other members of that proverbial field, but his career statistics speak for themselves. In fact, if I didn't know any better, I'd find them pretty hard to believe.

On the way home from school one afternoon in the mid-1990s, I remember telling my mum that I'd learnt that day that the oldest person in the world was three-hundred-and-something years old.
'I don't think that's true,' she said calmly. 'I think the oldest person is a little over 100.'
But I was adamant.
'Mum,' I stubbornly insisted. 'You're wrong! Somebody told me at school that there's a person who is more than 300 years old!'

I don't know the who, why or how that led me to this belief, but in hindsight it's safe to say that five-year-old me didn't have much of a leg to stand on. Maybe I was a particularly stubborn and gullible child, but I doubt that my mother is the only parent in the world to hear something outlandish come out of the mouth of their kid. After all, children are pretty impressionable. If somebody tells them something, they'll probably believe it without too much questioning. That's why they're able to be so easily convinced to believe in Santa, the Easter Bunny and Don Bradman.

For at least the first few years of my life, I didn't really question the existence of any of these things. Santa came down our chimney to give us either presents or coal once a year, the Easter Bunny gave us chocolate to celebrate Jesus, and Don Bradman was nearly twice as good as any other cricketer in history. Maybe his career statistics aren't quite as far-fetched as the idea of Santa or the Easter Bunny, nor the concept of someone living for over 300 years, but to be honest, they aren't all that far off.

Every kid growing up in Australia knows the story – or at least within the sports-obsessed bubble in which I spent my early days they did. Don Bradman, definitely the greatest batter, almost certainly the greatest cricketer, and probably the greatest sportsperson to ever live, averaged 99.94 runs per innings over the course of his career, while all the other really good players in the game's history averaged around 50 or so.

To cricket fans it's such common knowledge that the numbers hold little shock value. Non-cricket fans probably have no idea what it means, and if you're a stats lover who falls into this category, boy oh boy are you in for a treat. But before we dive too deep into the numbers, let's go back to the beginning.

Bradman was born way back in 1908 in a little town called Cootamundra in New South Wales. A little after his second birthday, his family moved to Bowral, into a house with what has since become arguably the most famous water tank in the world.

As a young boy, Don liked to spend his afternoons throwing a golf ball against the curved bricks which surrounded this water tank and whacking the rebounds with a single cricket stump. Maybe this was a result of the boredom that invariably came with being a child in the small town of Bowral, but if you ask me it sounds like a pretty great way to pass the time. Whatever Don's reasons, it helped him to develop some impressive hand-eye coordination, and with a significantly bigger bat in his hand and a cricket ball which behaved a little more predictably than his golf ball, he unsurprisingly excelled.

In late 1928, when he was 20 years old, Bradman was selected for his first ever international appearance after a few handy performances playing for New South Wales in Australia's domestic leagues. He struggled, making just 1 and 18 as his Australian side lost by what was and still is a record margin of 675 runs to their old foe England. Not a great start, and Don was dropped from the side for the next match.

After another eye-catching performance for New South Wales he was recalled for the third Test. Though England would go on to win the game and with it the four-match series, Bradman endeared himself to the selectors with scores of 79 and 112, and he would never look back.

By 1932, a 24-year-old Bradman had already put together some sort of career, and had shown a particular penchant for accumulating mammoth scores. Despite having only played at the international level for four years, he had scored a double-century on six occasions, a number which only six other players in the almost-150-year history of cricket have bettered in their entire careers.

It was in this year that the infamous bodyline series took place, a series in which some dubious but undoubtedly effective bowling tactics by England saw the averages of virtually every Australian batter plummet. Bradman was no exception, averaging 56.57 – a number just over half of what he would go on to average for his entire career, but which is still superior to the career averages of most of the greatest batters of all time.

That series would be the biggest, and only, blip on a pretty flawless career. He resumed his normal exploits immediately after, playing for another 16 years – albeit with a lengthy hiatus while the world dealt with WWII – and ultimately leading one of the most successful teams in the game's history. He wound things up in 1948, with his final innings coming against an English side which he had spent much of the two prior decades terrorising.

As he walked out to bat for the final time, Bradman's career average sat at 101.39. He needed just four runs to finish his career with an average in excess of 100 – an entirely arbitrary achievement but one which everyone no doubt wanted him to reach regardless, such is the fun of statistics. Clearly the odds were in his favour, but unfortunately he was bowled without scoring by a leg-spinner called Eric Hollies who will forever be remembered more for that wicket than his actual career. The legend goes that a tear in the great batter's eye hindered his ability to see the ball, but given that he would've batted again had the Aussies not ultimately demolished the Poms by an innings and 149 runs, that seems unlikely.

Despite that failure, Bradman still appeared to have plenty to give when he pulled up stumps at the ripe old age of 40. In fact, his final calendar year was the most prolific of his career in terms of total runs scored, and though that was largely attributable to the number of games he played, an average of 113.89 that year suggests he was still seeing the ball reasonably well.

But while that wasn't quite enough to remain in triple figures, he still ended his career with an extraordinary, ridiculous and borderline unbelievable average of 99.94. As the following graph shows, that's a lot more than everyone else to have ever played the game. The graph includes the batting average of every player in Test history to have played at least 20 innings (an oft-used cut-off point in cricket stats to weed out those who only played a handful of games). As you can see, there's a heavy concentration of players from an average of 15 through to around 40, though a large number of those are the batting averages of bowlers. Batters who manage to carve out reasonably long careers generally average over 40, with the very best making it into the 50s. At the time of writing the number of players who have managed to surpass an average of 50 is just 41 – that's in close to one-and-a-half centuries of cricket – while just five of those have crept over 60. The arrows allude to this with some vague categorisations of subpar, decent and elite batters, while the one on the far right simply points to Bradman's average because if it wasn't there, you probably wouldn't even notice his data point.

SPORT'S GREATEST STATISTICAL ANOMALIES

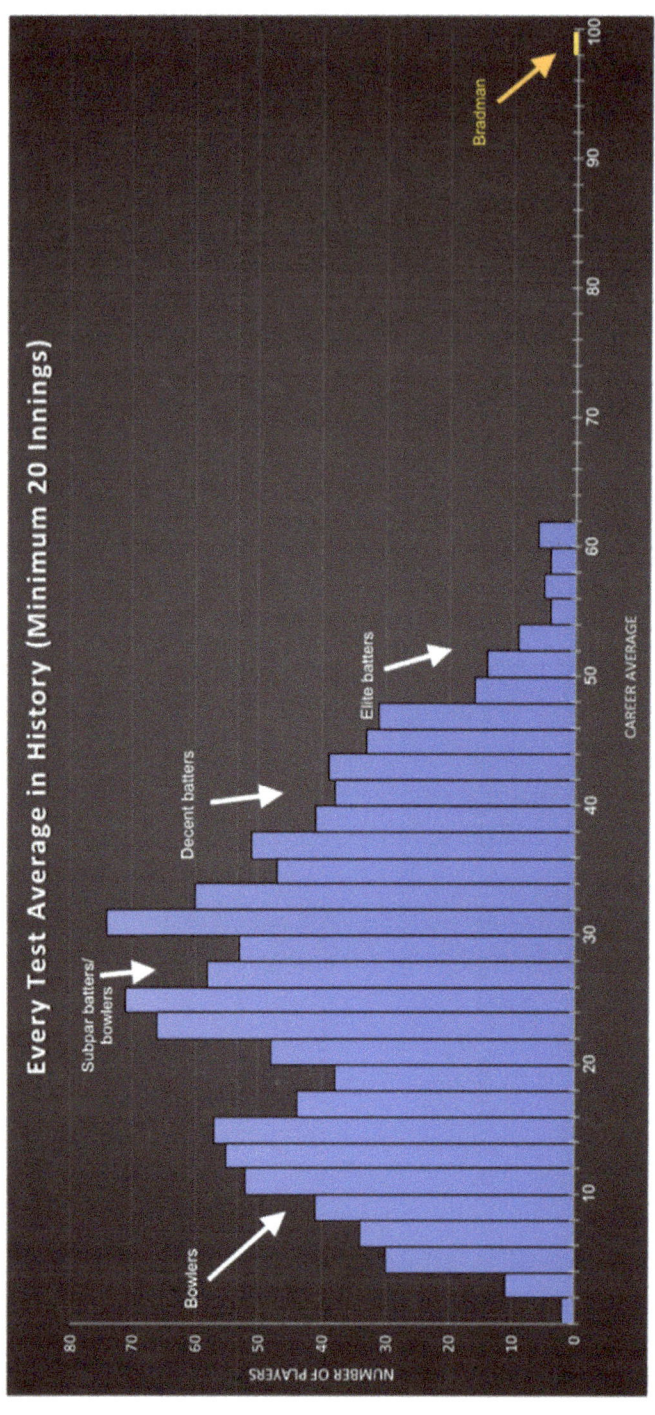

And remember – this is a graph about averages. Without wanting to minimise the feats of the likes of a Michael Phelps or Kelly Slater and subsequently undermine the entire premise of this book, their achievements were a result of an accumulation of victories over the course of their careers. They accumulated those wins far more quickly than everyone else, but they only had to beat their opponents by a solitary point, millisecond or whatever it may have been to earn the victory. Bradman's *average* innings was well over 1.5 times better than anyone else in the game's history, and close to twice that of many of the game's greatest ever players. His career would be equivalent to Michael Phelps winning the 200-metre butterfly by over a minute.

To stick to cricket references, an equally anomalous achievement would be a bowler averaging a little under 13 over the course of an extended career, or bowling at around 240 km/h. In everyday life, if a person stood at about 3.5 metres tall, or lived until they were 180, they would be able to lay claim to being as good as Bradman was at batting at being tall, or old.

And what's more, in cricket, more than in most other sports, statistics are a very direct indicator of performance. In basketball, a player might have 30 points on a given night but took 40 shots to get there and didn't play any defence, and subsequently more likely contributed to their team losing rather than winning. In cricket, and particularly in Test cricket, if you score a hundred you score a hundred. If you get five wickets, you get five wickets. You might get dropped a couple of times en route to that hundred, or get a couple of lucky wickets in an individual innings, but over the course of a career stats are a very reliable measure.

By the time his career wound up, Bradman had been playing at the top level for two decades, but while he accumulated a solid number of matches in that time, his 52 Tests and 80 innings pale in comparison to many of his modern-day counterparts. As a result, you'd probably imagine that his cumulative numbers would be uncompetitive with most of those players, but you'd be wrong. He ended his career with 6,996 runs, a number which sees him surrounded by great contemporaries like Sanath Jayasuriya, Mark Taylor, Andrew Strauss, David Boon and Sourav Ganguly, each of whom played in over 100 Tests.

Bradman's 12 double centuries are the most in the history of Test cricket, and every other player to have scored five or more played at least 85 matches. No player who played less Tests than Bradman has scored more than two double centuries in their career. This is outlined in the graph below, which includes all 39 players who managed to surpass 200 runs in an innings on at least three occasions in the first 145 years of Test cricket. The height of each data point represents the number of times that player walked out to bat, while their position on the x-axis denotes how many double centuries they scored.

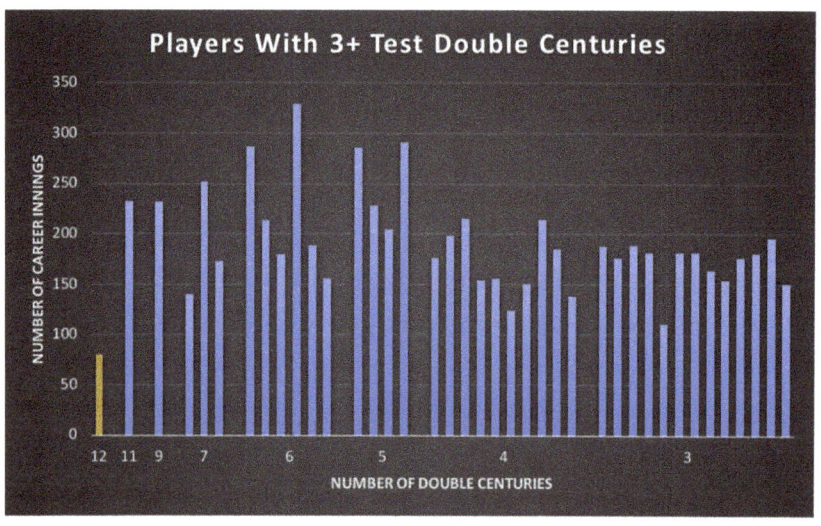

On average, the height of each bar should trend downwards as we head towards the right-hand side of the above graph, and had I included the multitude of players who have scored either one or two double centuries that would be even more evident. After all, more innings = more opportunities for big scores. Bradman, of course, is the clear outlier, sitting out there on the left with the most double centuries in history despite having played less than half the innings of the majority of players with whom he shares the graph.

For scores of 100+ the numbers are perhaps a little less startling, but nonetheless help to paint a picture of just what an extraordinary talent the man was. He sits 14th of all time in this statistic, though once he again he is surrounded by players who dwarf him in terms of matches and innings played. In fact, of all the players above him, no one has played less than 103 Tests (remember, Bradman played 52) or 184 innings (Bradman played 80). There are a couple hunting him down who could change that in the coming years in Virat Kohli and, in particular, Steve Smith, but they will still have played significantly more games than Bradman if and when they pass him.

If we tweak the stats a little, we can still get a pretty good feel for how prolific a century scorer Bradman was. The below graph looks at the average number of innings per century for every player who scored triple figures on at least 20 occasions up until September of 2022 (46 players). For example, if a player scored 20 centuries in 200 innings, they would be going at a rate of one century every ten innings.

SPORT'S GREATEST STATISTICAL ANOMALIES

If you follow cricket, you will recognise the vast majority of the above names. They are the absolute best of the best, the most highly regarded batters in cricket history, and their rate of centuries is pretty consistent. The bulk of them slot in at a century every six to eight innings, with a few creeping above and exactly two creeping below that number. One of those is Steve Smith, who is still in the process of carving out an unbelievable career and, after his first 85 Test matches, had scored a century every 5.59 innings. This is a significantly better rate than any of his predecessors with the exception, of course, of Don Bradman, who scored a century every 2.76 innings, comfortably more than twice as often as any other player on the above graph and marginally more than twice as often as Smith.

Smith, incidentally, is quickly writing his name into the record books as one of the greatest to ever play the game. An average of roughly 60 with the volume of innings he has already compiled at the age of just 32 means he will invariably go down in the top handful of run scorers in the game's history. Yet his average of around 60 is just – you guessed it – about 60% of Bradman's average. If you wiped 40 – the gap between he and Bradman – off Smith's average you'd come to around 20, a number not even close to sufficient to get you a game for any decent national side in world cricket.

One final statistic about Bradman's century-making prowess of note relates to his ability to convert half-centuries into centuries. Typically this is a mark of the great players – once they are established at the crease, they are very difficult to get out. Despite that, it's virtually unheard of for a batter to convert more than half of these scores of 50+ into triple figures. Of the names on the above graph – aside from Bradman of course – Matthew Hayden, Michael Clarke and Mohammad Azharuddin are the only ones to do it, each of them having scored one more century than half-centuries. Everyone else has more 50s than 100s, and often significantly more. Bradman's 29 100s were accompanied by just 13 50s, meaning that when he surpassed the 50-mark, there was a roughly 69% chance that he would be putting together a triple-figure score. Demoralising for the opposition to say the least.

So how did this all happen? How did one man become so much better than everyone else to have ever played the game? In many of the chapters in this book, there are mitigating factors which can help to explain, at least to an extent, how certain anomalies occurred. So what's Bradman's excuse?

Perhaps it's a product of the era, you might suggest. Maybe it was easier to make consistently high scores back then. Maybe the bowling wasn't as good. Maybe. And while it's true that there was a wealth of prospering batters around the same time – the likes of Herbert Sutcliffe (average of 60.73), Wally Hammond (average of 58.45) and Jack Hobbs (average of 56.94) – they didn't go close to averaging 99.94. And of the guys in Bradman's team, those who were facing the same bowlers as him? Aside from Jack Ryder, who averaged 51.62 over a relatively small sample size and shared the field just four times with Don, no one else managed to average even a half-century! Bill Ponsford, widely regarded as a brilliant player in his time, was the closest of Bradman's regular teammates with an average of 48.22, less than half that of Bradman's.

So what else could explain it? Of course, statistical variance is far more likely when there's less data, so had he not played for very long that would be a significant mitigating factor. But as already mentioned, he played international cricket for 20 years. That included a seven-year hiatus during the war and they didn't play as much cricket as they do today back then, so his 52 Tests don't compete with the most played these days, but it's still more than enough to

exclude the possibility that his stats are purely a product of him not playing many matches.

The reality is, there is no explanation. There is no single reason to explain why this man was so, so, so much better than anyone else in the history of this sport. A combination of extreme talent, plenty of practice at a young age and a whole lot of hard work and dedication are contributing factors, but they're factors which probably apply to most players who make it to the international level – and many who don't. The simple fact is, the man was a freak, and even that doesn't seem to do justice to do the anomaly that was his career. Cricinfo, the most reliable authority on all things cricket, perhaps explained it best:

> *"Unquestionably the greatest batsman in the game, arguably the greatest cricketer ever, and one of the finest sportsmen of all time, Don Bradman was so far ahead of the competition as to render comparisons meaningless and to transcend the game he graced."*

And even this falls short; arguably the greatest cricketer ever? Please. There have and will be plenty of other incredible players in the game's history, but none will ever come close to matching the feats of Don Bradman, the greatest statistical anomaly in all of sports.

Bradman died peacefully at his Adelaide home in February of 2001, a few years younger than his career batting average. Normally this would be tragic, the sign of a life cut short. Bradman was 92.

SPORT'S GREATEST STATISTICAL ANOMALIES

By the Numbers

- Bradman averaged **99.94 runs per innings** throughout his career. The **second highest average ever is 61.87.**

- Bradman **scored a century on average once every 2.759 innings;** Steve Smith is the second most frequent century scorer in history with **one every 5.59 innings at the time of writing,** and no other batter to have scored at least 20 centuries has a number of **less than 6**.

- Bradman scored the **most ever Test double centuries with 12 in 80 innings.** Every other player to score even **3 or more double centuries has done so in 111 innings or more**, while every other player to score **6 or more double centuries has done so in 140 innings or more**.

9

Basketball Career: John Stockton

When the Utah Jazz selected John Stockton with their 16th pick in the 1984 NBA draft, the 2,000 attendees at the Salt Palace, a convention centre in Salt Lake City, responded with silence. Normally there are cheers, or at the very least a smattering of polite applause. Occasionally, disgruntled fans will even make their displeasure known with a chorus of boos. But this crowd didn't make a peep.

For most of his college career Stockton had been relatively unheralded, and though his stock had risen a ton in the leadup to the NBA draft courtesy of a terrific final season at Gonzaga, the pick came as a huge surprise. There wasn't a consensus by any means about who the Jazz would take with their 16th pick, but there were a handful of names who seemed likely. John Stockton wasn't one of them.

The state of Utah's perception of the 6'1" point guard from Gonzaga was about as indistinct as the below picture of him, taken out of local newspaper *The Deseret News* the day after Stockton was drafted. According to that article, 'pre-dinner blessings are noisier' than the crowd's response – not the first comparison I would have thought of, but probably an apt simile for the state of Mormons.

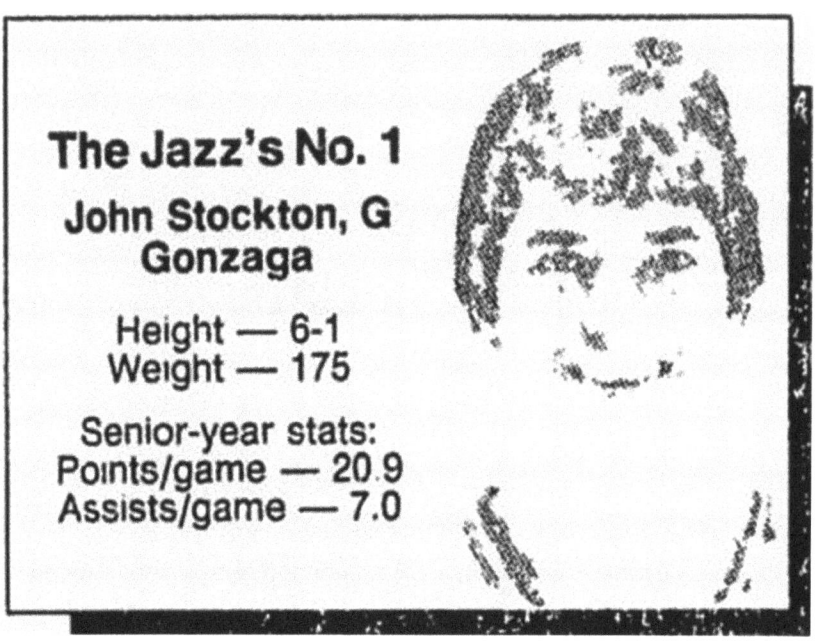

Fast forward 20 years, and a statue outside the Jazz's home stadium which far more closely resembles Stockton than the above picture would greet fans on arrival. The statue fittingly stands alongside that of Stockton's long-time teammate and one of the game's greatest ever players, Karl Malone, and depicts him doing what it was that he did better than almost anyone else in NBA history; passing.

The art of passing is one which is typically best personified by a team's point guard, though in the age of position-less basketball it is not unusual to see forwards and centres who are more than capable of facilitating for their teammates. In contrast to the Lebrons and Jokics of the world, Stockton was the epitome of a traditional

BASKETBALL CAREER: JOHN STOCKTON

point guard. With a diminutive stature – at least in NBA terms – he was nothing out of the ordinary as an athlete, and at no point in his career would he become anything more than a reasonable scorer either. But when it came to organising his team's offence and setting up teammates, there have been few better.

Over the first three years of his career, Stockton predominantly came off the bench for the Jazz. His passing numbers were impressive enough though, and encouragingly improved every year – from 5.1 assists per game in his rookie year up to 8.2 in his third season. But while his assist numbers were indicative of his promise, he struggled to do much scoring himself, failing to average more than eight points per game in any individual season.

In the 1987/88 season, that promise manifested into something more tangible. Stockton was moved into a starter's role, starting in 79 of 82 regular season games compared to just two the season prior. Alongside Karl Malone, he helped lead the Jazz to a 47-win season – the best in franchise history to that point – and began his march towards statistical domination.

Not only did his scoring numbers nearly double, but more importantly he averaged a whopping 13.8 assists that year, which would be the first of nine successive seasons which he ended as the league-leader in that category. That average of 13.8 assists per game is still the fourth highest in league history; first, second, fifth and sixth also belong to Stockton on that list, with all five of those seasons occurring consecutively between 1987 and 1992.

You won't be surprised to learn that during the course of this spectacular statistical career, Stockton became the all-time assists leader. Needing 11 assists to break the record against the Denver Nuggets in a game early in 1995, he achieved the feat after a little less than a quarter and a half. That's a whole lot of assists in 18 minutes of basketball.

Incredibly, when he broke that record Stockton was only a little over halfway through his career, with that game against the Nuggets occurring in his 11th season as an NBA player. He would go on to play 19.

9,922 was the number of assists he needed to break the record back in '95, and by the end of his career in 2003 he had added nearly 6,000 more to finish with 15,806 in total. At this time, Mark Jackson was second with 10,215, giving Stockton a lead of almost 55% over everyone else to have ever played. The numbers of many of the greatest point guards of all time pale in comparison – Magic Johnson had a comparatively measly total of 10,141, while the Big O, Oscar Robertson, ended with 9,887.

His lead today is still gargantuan, but it has dwindled somewhat in the years following his retirement courtesy largely of a talented point guard a little over ten years his junior, who had already begun carving out what would become an historic career when Stockton hung up the boots. Jason Kidd, having just turned 30 when Stockton retired in 2003, still had ten years left in his long career, and would ultimately end up slotting into second position in all-time assists as of today. He put up some incredible numbers; in total, Kidd played 19 seasons, and after averaging 7.7 dimes per game in his rookie year, averaged at least eight every season of his career until the final two. This consistent, sustained high-level performance was enough to see him accumulate 12,091 assists. It's a huge number, and was for a long time close to 2,000 more than third place, but is still just a tick over 75% of what Stockton managed.

In fact, taking a look at Jason Kidd's career is perhaps the best way to understand just how anomalous Stockton's numbers are. Between

1995 and 2010, Kidd finished in the top five for assists per game in every single season. In five of those seasons he finished with the most assists per game in the league. That's a long time at the top.

Of course, assist averages don't take into account how many games a player plays, so aren't necessarily the best indicator for totals. But while Kidd drops down the list for a couple of his seasons when evaluating his raw totals as opposed to his averages, he still managed to finish in the top five for total assists in 12 of the 15 seasons mentioned above. He wasn't the most durable player in history, but nor did he have a career marred by injury. In fact, the 1,391 games he played was good enough for the 12th most in league history.

For all intents and purposes, it's a resume befitting an all-time assists leader. But while he did wind up dropping more dimes – and pretty comfortably too – than everyone with the exception of John Stockton over the course of his career, he still fell so far short of reaching the record. For comparison, Kidd was like a swimmer trying to break Michael Phelps' 200m freestyle record of 1.42.96 swimming it in about 2.15. He'd be the swimmer from that minnow nation over in lane one, turning for his final lap as Phelps touched the wall 50 metres away.

Except in this conversation, that minnow nation representative is the second-best swimmer of all time. And he's a basketballer not a swimmer, and Michael Phelps is actually John Stockton. Make sense?

Incidentally, at the time of writing, Chris Paul, the man known as the Point God, is doing a good job of chasing down Kidd and potentially even getting significantly closer to Stockton, subsequently ruining the premise of this chapter in the process. At the conclusion of the

2021/22 regular season he had clocked up 10,977 assists, and at the ripe old age of nearly 37 isn't showing many signs of slowing down. Continuing at the same rate of assists as he had in '21/22, he could expect to pass Kidd in about a season and half. It's looking increasingly likely that he'll be able to work his way into second spot, but it's still nearly impossible that he'll get even close to Stockton – to do so he'll need to play at the same level for roughly another six or seven years, at which point he'll be well into his 40s.

Like Stockton, Paul has been a terrific passer with elite court vision and an innate ability to hit the open man. What helped Stockton gain such a significant advantage over his peers in assist totals, however, was his incredible durability. At the end of his 17th season, Paul had accumulated a fairly healthy 1,157 games, but that was still 183 shy of what Stockton had managed to the same point in his career. Two seasons later, the Jazz legend had added another 164 to his total to work his way into fifth place of all-time in games played.

In 12 of his first 13 seasons, Stockton didn't miss a game, and he ended up playing all 82 regular season games in 16 of his 19 seasons in the league – and in one of those three in which he didn't, he played all 50 in a season shortened by a lockout. In those seasons, he led the league in assists per game on nine occasions, and was in the top five on another five.

For comparison, during those years where he was either leading or going close to leading the league in dimes, Kidd was averaging around eight or nine per game and accumulating 7-800 in total per season; Paul similar during his peak years. In contrast, at his best Stockton was averaging closer to 14, seeing him eclipse the 1,000 mark for total assists in a season a remarkable seven times. The four seasons with the most assists in NBA history all belong to him, as do seven of the top nine.

BASKETBALL CAREER: JOHN STOCKTON

The below graph highlights this dominance, showing every season in NBA/ABA history in which a player accumulated at least 900 assists. This has only happened 25 times, of which nine can be attributed to Stockton. His seasons are highlighted in purple.

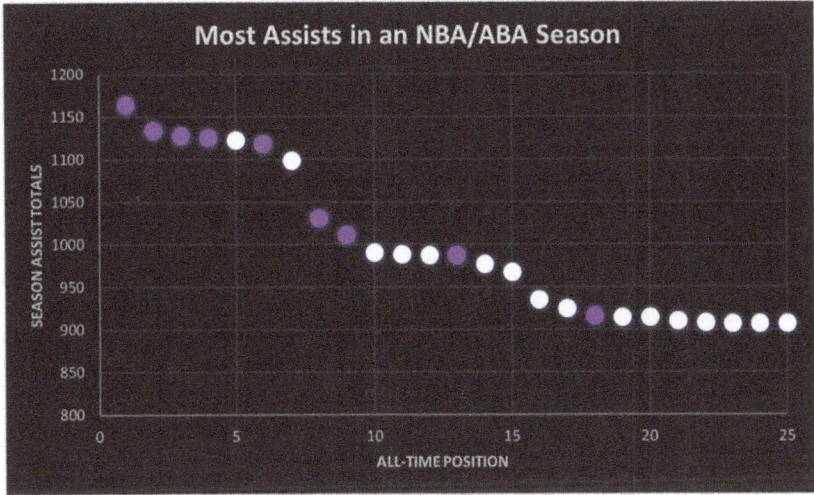

This consistent accumulation of so many of the league's best ever seasons in terms of assists is what has enabled him to develop such a hefty lead over his competition. Add to the mix his extraordinary durability, and you have a recipe for career-long statistical dominance. The below graph gives a visual look at just how far ahead of his rivals he is.

SPORT'S GREATEST STATISTICAL ANOMALIES

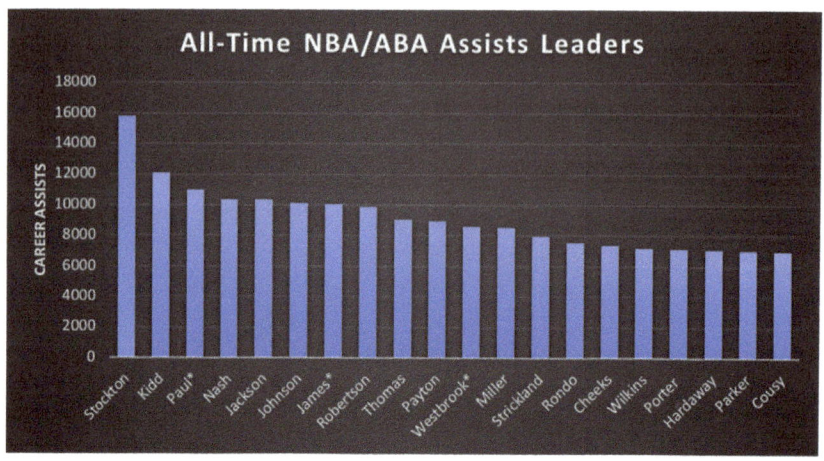

The difference between Stockton and Kidd is greater than the difference between Kidd and Andre Miller, who sits in 12th in all-time assists, while the difference between Stockton and fourth-placed Steve Nash takes us back to Mark Price, who sits in 76th and comfortably out of the picture on the above graph.

It's worth noting that, as is the case for many American sports, the NBA doesn't include playoffs in career statistics, so this metric only factors in the assists these players accumulated during the regular season. If you do add in playoffs, Stockton's lead only grows. Magic Johnson is a relatively comfortable post-season leader in assists while LeBron James moved into second just prior to writing as he continues his quest to lead every statistical category in existence by the end of his career; in third place is Stockton with 1,839, before a gap of nearly 600 follows back to Kidd in fourth. Add these numbers on top of the above graph, and Stockton's career total would sit at 17,645, with Kidd back in second on 13,354.

No matter how you cut the data, it's clear that Stockton was an assist machine, the best accumulator of this statistic in the game's history, and he combined it with incredible longevity to create a record that will likely never be matched.

Funnily enough, assists isn't the only statistical category that Stockton leads by far more than anyone reasonably should. Courtesy of the huge number of games he played and a willingness to try a lot harder on defence than many talented offensive guards, he racked up 3,265 steals over the course of his near two-decade long career. Coming in second is, once again, Jason Kidd, who managed 2,684 – a little over 80% of Stockton's number. The difference between Stockton and Kidd is around the same as the difference between Kidd and 13th place, which incidentally is a position owned by Stockton's favourite teammate – Karl Malone.

It's not quite as big a gap as that which he owns in assists and is also a little more niche, so probably less impressive, but nonetheless it's a noteworthy stat. That he owns such a commanding lead in two of the five major statistical categories is testament not only to his ability, but also to his durability and consistency. Indeed, a recent ESPN ranking on the top 74 NBA players of all time (this was a celebration of the NBA's 74th anniversary, so this number is a little less arbitrary than it sounds) placed Stockton at 28, labelling him 'unparalleled' in the latter of these traits.

But while this goes some way to recognising his feats, Stockton is still viewed by many as vastly underappreciated. Why? One reason is probably that he spent virtually the entirety of his career as the second-best player on his team. Karl Malone, whose career spanned almost exactly the same years as Stockton's, falls short only of Kareem Abdul-Jabbar and LeBron James in all-time points, with a significant proportion of those coming courtesy of his friend at the point guard position. Some argue that Stockton wouldn't have ended up with near the number of career assists he did if it wasn't for Malone draining 25 points per game, but plenty of others argue that Malone wouldn't have been eating so well if Stockton wasn't consistently serving up shots on a platter.

But alas, we will never know. Most likely it's a little from column A and a little from column B, but a large part of basketball is understanding how to play with the pieces around you, and it's safe to say Malone and Stockton certainly did that.

Unfortunately for the two of them, many of their Jazz team's prime years came when Michael Jordan and his Chicago Bulls were winning championships for fun, and despite accumulating plenty of hugely impressive statistics, they were never able to achieve the ultimate goal of winning the NBA Finals. Most likely, that's a major reason why so many underappreciate Stockton's career – the correlation between winning championships and getting recognition in the NBA must be as high as in just about any other league around the world. For the stats buffs out there, however, he's hard to miss.

BASKETBALL CAREER: JOHN STOCKTON

By the Numbers

- Stockton recorded **15,806 assists** throughout the course of his career. Jason Kidd sits in **second place of all-time with 12,091**, just **76.5% of Stockton's total**.

- Stockton has the **4 most prolific seasons in NBA/ABA history in terms of total assists**, as well as **5 of the top 6 and 7 of the top 9.**

- The gap in career totals between **Stockton and 2nd-placed Kidd is the same as between Kidd and 12th**, while the gap between **Stockton and 4th place is the same as the gap between 4th and 76th**.

10

Tennis Careers: The Big Three (Rafael Nadal, Novak Djokovic, Roger Federer)

DEBATE SURROUNDING THE 'Greatest of All Time', also known as the GOAT, permeates conversation in many sports around the globe. Often, it causes a great deal of controversy and probably an undue amount of frustration among indignant fans, who seem to take the prospect of a stranger on the internet thinking that one extremely talented player was marginally better than another very personally.

This is pretty normal (the conversation…the frustration less so) and happens across many sports – you need only look to the NBA for an example, where the LeBron vs Jordan debate has become hotter with every year into his 30s that LeBron has continued to dominate. What is abnormal, however, is when this discussion surrounds three players who have played in the same era – which is exactly what has happened in the tennis world over the first couple of decades of this century.

Early in 2022, Rafael Nadal took out his 21st Grand Slam title. In doing so, he became the outright most successful male tennis player at Grand Slams in history, breaking a three-way tie on 20. Sitting alongside him on that number had been Novak Djokovic and Roger Federer, both of whose career timelines have closely aligned with that of Nadal. Nobody else has won more than 14.

By the time the last of that year's four Grand Slams were completed, Nadal had taken his total to 22 and Djokovic to 21. Federer, aged 41, finally retired in September, but with the other two still going strong there's every chance that in the years to come they will continue to extend this lead over every other man to ever have picked up a racquet. The supremacy of a trio playing out their careers simultaneously is unprecedented, and is outlined in the graph below.

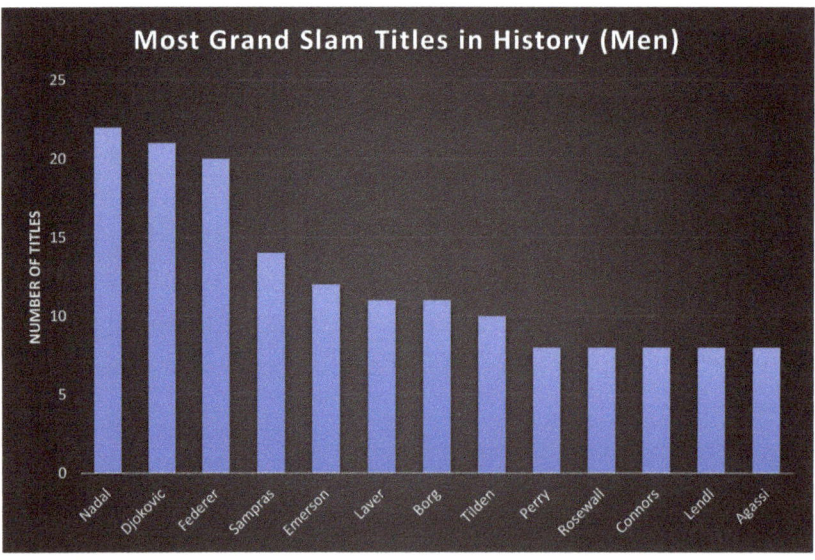

Federer was the first of the three on the scene, and collected his first Grand Slam way back in 2003 at Wimbledon. Inclusive of that tournament, 77 majors were played on the ATP Tour up until September of 2022 – The Big Three won 63 of them. This means that they accumulated 81.82% of the Grand Slams available to them over the course of almost 19 years. The three virtually held a monopoly over the biggest events on the tennis calendar for close to 20 years, denying the likes of poor old Andy Murray from winning anywhere near as many as he deserved.

Murray, incidentally, offers an excellent reference point for the dominance of our trio. He carried the hopes of success-starved tennis fans in Britain for almost 15 years, setting up shop as the fourth-ranked tennis player in the world for seemingly his entire career. In that time he made 21 semi-finals appearances and 11 finals appearances at major tournaments for just three Grand Slam titles. Of the eight finals he lost, all eight came at the hands of one of The Big Three. And of his ten semi-final losses? The first was to Andy Roddick and the last to Stan Wawrinka – the eight sandwiched in between were to Federer, Nadal or Djokovic. Poor Andy. In literally any other era before and most likely after this one, you'd think a guy who was better at the sport than all of his competitors with the exception of the three best players ever would enjoy a little more Grand Slam success, but he ended his career with just three majors to his name – certainly no mean feat, but likely a lot less than he would have won had he been playing at another time.

Which brings me to a point which makes the trio of Federer, Nadal and Djokovic even more fascinating: while they were busy denying Andy Murray and co from winning their fair share of tournaments, they were also busy denying one another. Each of them would almost undoubtedly have won plenty more tournaments were they not forced to share the spoils among each other.

Take Federer, as an example. The Swiss Maestro's 20 Grand Slam victories to date have been accompanied by 11 Grand Slam final losses. Here's a chronological list of the players who beat him in those finals: Nadal, Nadal, Nadal, Nadal, Nadal, Juan Martin del Potro, Nadal, Djokovic, Djokovic, Djokovic, Djokovic.

It's the same deal for Rafa. Up until the end of 2022 he lost eight Grand Slam finals to go with his 22 victories – those losses came against Federer, Federer, Djokovic, Djokovic, Djokovic, Stan Wawrinka, Federer, and Djokovic. And Djokovic himself? Well he actually ruins this line of argument a little, but even so six of his 11 Grand Slam final defeats thus far have come at the hands of either Federer or Nadal (two others were against Murray – go Andy!), so it's safe to assume he could've had a couple more if they weren't around.

Unsurprisingly, there are literally no comparable eras in the history of the game. Back in the '60s Aussie duo Roy Emerson and Rod Laver had to share the spoils a little, winning 23 Grand Slams between them throughout the course of the decade, but they a) were only two people, b) didn't win at even near the rate of The Big Three, c) only did it for a decade and d) would have been playing within a far smaller pool of professional tennis players.

More recently you've got Pete Sampras and Andre Agassi winning 21 Slams between them in a touch over ten years, and Bjorn Borg, Jimmy Connors and John McEnroe sharing 26 within a relatively short time frame, but nothing which goes close to matching either the level of dominance nor the length for which it was sustained by The Big Three.

For reference, the second most Grand Slams won by a group of three players over the course of 77 of them being played, or a little over 19 years – the length of time since Federer kicked off the nearly 82% winning streak he has enjoyed with Nadal and Djokovic – is 31. That record – just under half of how many The Big Three won in the same duration – belongs to two trios; that of Rod Laver, Roy Emerson and Björn Borg, as well as that of Laver, Emerson and Ken Rosewall. Pete Sampras, Ivan Lendl and Andre Agassi sit one behind with 30 Grand Slam wins in the allotted time period. As mentioned, however, Laver and Emerson – along with Rosewall – won the vast majority of their major titles back in the '60s, before what's known as the Open Era (when tennis turned professional) began. Clearly they were still terrific players, but the level and depth of competition is generally viewed to have improved significantly since this time, meaning back then it was probably more likely for a handful of players to monopolise tournament wins.

Borg also didn't start winning Slams until years after Laver and Emerson had stopped, while a similar difference exists in the case of the more recent trio. Lendl's career was winding to a close as those of Agassi and Sampras were beginning, and his last Grand Slam win came before the first of both the other two. As a result, the three were never really in direct competition. Agassi and Sampras certainly were, but not Lendl. None of these examples is a great comparison to The Big Three, which might not make for good reading but certainly helps to prove just how anomalous the supremacy of our three guys at one time really is.

In the women's game it's much the same. Most of the dominant players in history have largely enjoyed a period to themselves – Martina Navratilova won 15 of her 18 Grand Slam singles titles between 1981 and 1987 (though she did share this time with the latter stages of Chris Evert's period of success), Steffi Graf then came in and won her 22 between 1987 and 1999, before Serena Williams stepped right in to win the 23 she has won between 1999 and 2017. Margaret Court and Billie Jean King had a fun little battle from 1965 to 1973, winning 25 of the 36 in that time, but again that doesn't get close to the dominance nor longevity of The Big Three.

There's very little to explain why the careers of the three most successful players in the history of the men's game – and by some margin – happen to have taken place over virtually exactly the same period of time. Perhaps the best explanatory factor is an intangible one – that greatness motivates greatness, and the sustained excellence of the group pushes the individual to a higher level.

Djokovic, in the eyes of many, could certainly be seen to fit into this category. He was the latest to the party – Federer had already won 12 Grand Slams when he won his first while Nadal had won three, and those two won another ten between them before Novak won his second. By that stage – early 2011 – Djokovic was 23 years old and had been competing in Slams for six years, and to many he seemed destined for the kind of career that Andy Murray ultimately had. He was as good as anyone in the world with the exception of Federer and Nadal, but those two were acting as a roadblock to his ability to take the next step.

Indeed, prior to the 2011 Australian Open, which kick-started Djokovic's ascension into the game's top tier, Federer and Nadal were responsible for almost all of his losses in the final four of Grand Slams. Alongside his solitary victory to that point at the 2008 Australian Open, Novak had made two other Grand Slam finals – the 2007 US Open, which he lost in straight sets to the Fed, and the 2010 US Open, which he lost in four sets to Nadal. He'd also made another six Grand Slam semi-finals – one of these he lost to Tomas Berdych, the other five he lost to either Federer or Nadal.

They both seemed much more naturally gifted than he was – certainly Federer was, and Nadal's unique game style and penchant for the clay court made him a far bigger threat at Grand Slams than Djokovic. Djokovic always had excellent court coverage and a strong defensive game, but he nonetheless seemed a step behind the other two and destined for a career of what-ifs.

But he had other ideas. He won the 2011 Australian Open, then Wimbledon and the US Open in the same year, and would go on to win at least one Grand Slam each year for the next decade with the exception of 2017. For years he had been playing at a level which, in a world sans Federer and Nadal, would probably have been good enough for a number of Grand Slam titles and would have continued to be for years to come. With them around, however, it wasn't, and so he became the fittest man on the planet and started to beat them.

Of course, it would be naïve to think that Djokovic just had to try a bit harder to match it with the other two – he obviously needed a pretty hefty dose of talent to get there as well. Perhaps it wasn't as evident early in his career as it was with Federer and Nadal, and perhaps he does have a smidge less natural ability than they do, but he has still been a brilliant player regardless – they may just have served as a motivating factor for him to take his game to another level.

Federer also cited this concept early in 2021, noting that Djokovic helped to make him a better player and that the two tend to draw the best out of one another. Not that Federer needed a whole lot of help – he had already won more Grand Slams than every other male in tennis history by the time Djokovic became a regular winner at majors – but nonetheless his comments hint at the competitivity between the group which may have served to further their dominance.

In order to highlight this dominance I've put together the below table, which shows the winners of every men's Grand Slam tournament from 2003 – bearing in mind that Federer won his first at Wimbledon that year – up until the end of 2022. Tournaments which weren't won by Federer, Nadal or Djokovic, however, are left blank to highlight how rare an occasion that has been. As you can see, we're still left with a pretty full table.

SPORT'S GREATEST STATISTICAL ANOMALIES

	Australian Open	French Open	Wimbledon	US Open
2003			Roger Federer	
2004	Roger Federer		Roger Federer	Roger Federer
2005		Rafael Nadal	Roger Federer	Roger Federer
2006	Roger Federer	Rafael Nadal	Roger Federer	Roger Federer
2007	Roger Federer	Rafael Nadal	Roger Federer	Roger Federer
2008	Novak Djokovic	Rafael Nadal	Rafael Nadal	Roger Federer
2009	Rafael Nadal	Roger Federer	Roger Federer	
2010	Roger Federer	Rafael Nadal	Rafael Nadal	Rafael Nadal
2011	Novak Djokovic	Rafael Nadal	Novak Djokovic	Novak Djokovic
2012	Novak Djokovic	Rafael Nadal	Roger Federer	
2013	Novak Djokovic	Rafael Nadal		Rafael Nadal
2014		Rafael Nadal	Novak Djokovic	
2015	Novak Djokovic		Novak Djokovic	Novak Djokovic
2016	Novak Djokovic	Novak Djokovic		

TENNIS CAREERS: THE BIG THREE

	Australian Open	**French Open**	**Wimbledon**	**US Open**
2017	Roger Federer	Rafael Nadal	Roger Federer	Rafael Nadal
2018	Roger Federer	Rafael Nadal	Novak Djokovic	Novak Djokovic
2019	Novak Djokovic	Rafael Nadal	Novak Djokovic	Rafael Nadal
2020	Novak Djokovic	Rafael Nadal	N/A	
2021	Novak Djokovic	Novak Djokovic	Novak Djokovic	
2022	Rafael Nadal	Rafael Nadal	Novak Djokovic	

The longest streak of Grand Slam victories shared by the three came during an extraordinary period in which they won 18 consecutive Grand Slams between the 2005 French Open and the 2009 Wimbledon tournament. That's more than four years without anyone else winning one. Even more incredibly, after Juan Martin del Potro took out the 2009 US Open (you can probably guess who the other three semi-finalists were), the trio went on to win 11 more in a row, meaning they won 29 out of 30 successive major tournaments and that no one else aside from del Potro won a Grand Slam for close to eight years. Crazy.

And though they are no longer all at the peak of their powers, the collective dominance hasn't yet let up. The second most consecutive Grand Slams won by any one of the three is 13, a streak which ended with Dominic Thiem's win at the US Open in 2020. Following that, Nadal won the French Open (which took place after the US Open that year as a result of the pandemic), Djokovic three of the four

Grand Slams the next year, and he and Nadal shared three of the four in 2022. At well into their 30s and theoretically reaching the twilight of their sporting careers, they still managed to win 20 of the last 23 Grand Slam tournaments prior to this chapter being written.

That doesn't bode well for other talented players reaching the latter stages of their own careers. Grigor Dimitrov, for example, was lauded as a budding star early in his career and reached as high as number three in the world, but on numerous occasions had his quest for a maiden Grand Slam halted by one of The Big Three. At four years younger than Djokovic, the youngest member of the trio, Dimitrov could feasibly have hoped to enjoy some peak years without having to deal with the three greatest players in the game's history. Unfortunately, having turned 31 in 2022, he appears to be sliding towards the end of an unfulfilled career while Federer, Nadal and Djokovic walk at their own pace.

It's highly unlikely that we'll ever see anything like this current era of tennis in the game again. Certainly there'll be plenty more incredible players to play the game and some of their careers will probably overlap, but the likelihood of three of the best playing at the same time and winning almost all of the Grand Slams for close to two decades – and by the time their careers finish it may be more than that – is extremely slim. Aside from the motivation factor I've mentioned, there's very little to explain it. It's a fluke, a complete coincidence, and one of sport's great anomalies.

TENNIS CAREERS: THE BIG THREE

By the Numbers

- Nadal, Djokovic and Federer have won **22, 21 and 20 Grand Slams** respectively playing in the same era; **no other male has ever won more than 14**.

- In the 18 years from Wimbledon of 2003 until the Australian Open of 2022, one member of the trio won **63 of the 77 majors** played – a **total of 81.82%**.

- At one point between 2005 and 2012, one of the trio won **18 consecutive Grand Slams,** and **29 of 30**.

11

Soccer Team: Leicester City, 2015

As a passionate fan of Australian Rules Football and its top-level league, the AFL, I find it difficult to relate to supporters of the English Premier League (EPL), and indeed many soccer leagues around the world. Though I can't claim to know the ins and outs of every league of every sport around the globe, the AFL must be close to the top in terms of parity for all 18 clubs. Equalisation is at the forefront of a significant proportion of the decisions made by the powers that be, and within a ten-year cycle each club should theoretically have ample opportunity to enjoy some time at the top. It doesn't always work out exactly in that way, but the opportunities are there for all. It's sport's version of communism, but without the dictators.

So when I look at the EPL, the dominance of a select few teams is a stark contrast and something which is at times difficult to get my head around. In the 23 seasons between 1992, the first year of the Premier League as we know it today, and 2015, just five teams won the title, and on 22 of those occasions it was one of either Manchester United, Manchester City, Arsenal or Chelsea – Blackburn were the lone exception in 1994/95. It always makes me wonder – just how happy are fans of Manchester United when their side wins a 13th title in 20 years? My football team recently won three Premierships in five years and each was unequivocally less exciting than the one prior – by the 13th it must be pretty mundane. And what do fans of teams who have seemingly no hope of ever even competing with the powerhouses have to look forward to?

In 2016, Leicester City gave hope to fans of every single team in England with the exception of Manchester United, Arsenal, Liverpool, Chelsea and Manchester City – who already had plenty – when they won one of the most unlikely titles in the history of sport. The Foxes, as they're otherwise known, won relatively comfortably – finishing on 81 points, ten points ahead of second-placed Arsenal – and made the select few probably-not-very-good punters who put some cash on them at $5000-1 prior to the season very happy.

As an anomaly, this one isn't easy to define. It was a hugely unlikely occurrence – in fact it might be the most unlikely thing to ever happen in sport and perhaps even in life in general – but it's difficult to quantify exactly why. It just is. Leicester City didn't break any records or even really do anything statistically unlikely – they just won a very top-heavy league as a small club that would have realistically been happy at the start of the season to avoid relegation.

To find a comparison, I've scoured the archives to find an equivalent underdog, and stumbled across Norwich City about halfway through the 2019/20 English Premier League season. After 22 games, they were paying $4,500-1 to win the title – similar to Leicester City at the beginning of the 2015/16 season. At that point in time, Norwich City had scored 14 points from their 21 league matches and found themselves 47 points behind league-leaders Liverpool. The team affectionately known as The Canaries – who had to that point won three of their 21 matches – would have needed to, at a minimum, win 15 of their remaining 17 matches and draw the other two to have a chance at winning the title, assuming Liverpool lost all the rest of their games and every other team near the top of the table also lost a vast majority of theirs. It's safe to say the bookies were confident that wasn't a market they would have to pay out, and they were correct – Norwich City went on to lose all but three of their last 17 matches and finish in dead last, more than four wins behind the team one spot ahead of them.

Anyone who bets will know that typically, the bookies are pretty damn good at setting markets, so how did they get this one so wrong? The answer, in short, is that they were fully justified in pitting Leicester City as such a rank outsider – there was literally nothing to suggest The Foxes had any hope whatsoever of winning the league, and relegation was a far, far more likely outcome. In fact, that was paying just $3-1.

The club's fortunes in the lead-up to the 2015/16 season also suggested that relegation was very much on the cards – certainly more so than winning a Premier League title. Leicester City had been promoted to the top-level of English football, and what most believe is the best league in the world, a year earlier after they finished atop the Championship. It was their first appearance in the Premier League since 2004, and as is often the case, they struggled with the step-up.

With nine games left in the 2014/15 season they were in last place in the EPL, and relegation seemed probable. In an unlikely turnaround, however, they won seven of their last nine games and worked their way up to 14th. In answer to my earlier question about what teams with seemingly no chance of winning the title look forward to, this is probably a good example. Presumably fans were on cloud nine after their team of battlers managed to avoid finishing in the bottom three in a 20-team league. 14th was some sort of achievement!

As the odds suggested, however, it was more likely to be a delaying of the inevitable rather than the start of anything particularly exciting, and nothing in the off-season suggested they would be anything but a cellar dweller for another year in 2015/16. They got a new manager, Claudio Ranieri, but even he didn't have particularly high aspirations – he publicly claimed to be aiming for a whopping 40 league points, which would have been enough for them to escape relegation by the skin of their teeth.

It wasn't until seven games into the new season, however, that they lost their first game, which took their record to 3-3-1 and saw them sitting in sixth place on the league table. Woohoo! Go Leicester! Most probably saw it as a bit of a novelty, one of those quirks that arises in most leagues early in the season when a team finds itself significantly higher or lower than every sane person thinks they should be, and generally these sides regress to the mean as the season wears on. Leicester City did the opposite.

Perhaps the most important moment of the season came in their tenth match, when they held Crystal Palace scoreless for their first clean sheet of the season. Though they had already outperformed expectations to that point, they had been struggling to contain teams defensively, and so Ranieri, in an ingenious managerial move, promised them pizza after every match in which the opposition didn't score. They must have seriously enjoyed the feed, because after they filled their tummies with a bit of Italian following that victory they went on to become one of the stingiest defenses in the league, earning themselves 14 more pizzas through their remaining

28 matches. Ranieri most probably hadn't anticipated that and might have considered limiting his elite athletes to three or four slices per match some way through the season, but regardless, all of the pizza appeared to have no adverse effect as they went on to win the league without a hiccup.

It's difficult to define just how much of an outlier this is in sporting terms – there is no tangible way to determine how much more unlikely one team's championship was than another. To help out a little, I've charted the performance of every team promoted to the Premier League in the ten years prior to Leicester City over the two seasons following their promotion.

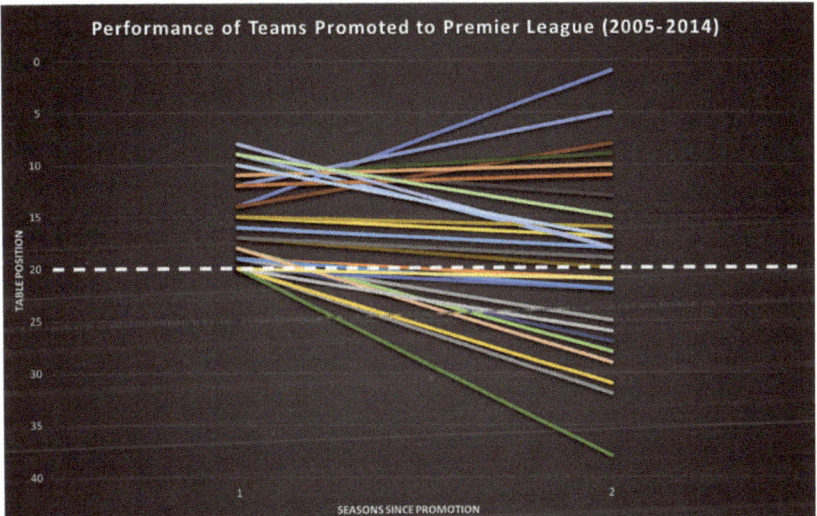

Leicester City, of course, is the navy blue line which pokes its head out at the top. The table positions go to 40 to include the teams which were relegated back to the Championship the year after their promotion, with the white dotted line indicating the end of the Premier League. The dark green line, for example, represents poor old Derby County, who finished in last place in the EPL in the first season following their 2007 promotion, then 18th in the Championship the year after.

They are comfortably the worst-performed team during the charted decade, but they are far from alone in terms of being relegated immediately after promotion. In fact, of the 30 teams included on the graph above, 12 finished in the bottom three in their first year in the EPL and were booted straight back to the Championship. Of the remaining 18, five more fell back the year after, meaning just a tick over 43% of promoted teams over a ten-year period managed to remain at the top level for more than two years. Clearly, winning the EPL isn't typically on the agenda for these teams.

And while there are a handful of teams who managed to sneak into the top ten throughout the 60 seasons noted above, on only two occasions have those teams finished in the top seven. One, of course, was Leicester City – the other was Newcastle. As you can see on the graph, this was pretty easily the second-best finish by a team in the two seasons following promotion during this time, but it still falls a long way short of the Foxes' effort.

Newcastle's fifth place finish came in 2011/12. The 65 points they managed that year was 16 points short of what Leicester managed in 2015/16, and saw them finish 24 points behind league-leaders Manchester City and Manchester United. Newcastle is also a perennial Premier League club. Where Leicester City had spent the ten years prior to promotion – and a large portion of their club history – at a lower level, Newcastle were promoted after winning the 2009/10 Championship, which was the first season since 1992/93 that they'd been out of the top league. Their trip to the Championship was just a blip in the history of what is generally a mid-tier Premier League club. Unlike Leicester City, they were simply returning to where they belong.

Leicester City, for what it's worth, seemed determined to prove the anomalous nature of their victory, failing to give much of a whimper the next season when they finished 12th. Over the ensuing few years they would remain a mid-tier Premier League team, and the first place next to their name in 2015/16 stands out as a relatively random occurrence.

Making it even more random is the way in which a champion is crowned in the Premier League. The aforementioned AFL, like in many different codes around the world, has a finals series to determine a winner. Eight teams out of 18 make it, and over four weeks they all try to make it to the Grand Final, where the team which wins on the day is crowned the Premier. Not an unusual concept, and one which plenty if not most sports and leagues worldwide use to determine the season's champion.

Not so in the Premier League, or indeed many soccer leagues around the world. They use what is probably a much more fair – and also a little less exciting – system, whereby the team which performs the best throughout the course of the 38-game season wins. This, of course, means that the best team over the entirety of the year is the winner, in contrast to a finals system which allows for the possibility of an inferior team simply playing well at the right time and on the grandest stage swooping in to take the glory.

As a result, outcomes like Leicester City's triumph are much less likely to ever occur. Tipped as a bottom side prior to the season, The Foxes didn't have to just sneak their way into the top half of the table and then hit form when it mattered most. They had to outperform experienced, dominant teams like Manchester United and Manchester City – who invariably finish in the top handful each year as a right – throughout the entire season.

It's an incredible achievement whichever way you look at it, but there is one small caveat worth mentioning. The 81 points which

Leicester City accumulated throughout that famous season would only have been enough to win three of the first 23 seasons following the turn of the century in the Premier League. Every other year the winner finished with more, and often so too did another team or two. This doesn't take a whole lot away from the achievement, but had we been in another season where a Manchester United or City put up closer to 90, as they have on many occasions, this chapter wouldn't exist and you would all be spending time with your families instead of reading about statistical anomalies. 81 points would be an impressive feat nonetheless, but finishing second or third with a high total wouldn't be viewed as one of the greatest achievements in sporting history. Of course, Leicester City contributed to the usually dominant teams failing to win as often by beating them, but that alone can't account for the fact that the second-placed side that year managed just 71 points.

Regardless, The Foxes beat the teams that were put in front of them and cruised to a comfortable victory, despite being roughly 1,500 times more likely to be relegated than to win the league, according to the betting odds. In fact, former Leicester striker Gary Lineker said that he wouldn't have even bothered placing a punt on them at odds of ten million to one because it would be a 'waste of a quid', such was the lack of confidence in the team, even from club icons. Incidentally, he also hosted his football show in his undies after they won on what is generally considered to be a reputable television network, the BBC, having made a promise which he presumably didn't anticipate having to keep five months before the end of the season.

And this, perhaps, is the best way to quantify just how anomalous the win was. There might not be numbers or statistics to explain how far apart from normality Leicester City's title stands, but if it was enough to warrant a BBC presenter hosting a show in his boxer shorts, it deserves its place in this book.

SOCCER TEAM: LEICESTER CITY, 2015

By the Numbers

- Leicester City won the Premier League in 2016 in their **2nd season after being promoted** from the Championship.

- No other team promoted between 2005 and 2014 finished **higher than 5th** within two seasons of being promoted.

- Just **13 of the 30 teams** promoted to the Premier League between 2005 and 2014 stayed there for more than two years, and of those, only **5 finished in the top 10** in that period.

12

Golf Season: Byron Nelson, 1945

WHEN MOST PEOPLE think of golfing legends, they think of names such as Tiger Woods, Jack Nicklaus and Happy Gilmore. The likes of Ben Hogan and Arnold Palmer are also fairly widely lauded in the sporting world, but there are numerous brilliant players who tend to slip under the radar outside of the more dedicated golfing community.

Byron Nelson is one such example. In the golfing world, his exploits don't slip under anything – he was the first player to have a PGA Tour event named after him, he's in the Hall of Fame yada yada yada – but for most, he isn't exactly a household name.

A major reason for this is simply time – Nelson, who was born in Texas in 1912, retired way back in 1946. His relatively short career – at least by golfing standards – lasted only 14 years, and was plagued by global struggles which transcended the game of golf. He turned pro while the world was in the midst of The Great

Depression, something which limited the number of high-profile tournaments that he was able to play in, while the final six years of his professional career took place during World War II.

The latter of these had a particularly significant impact on his career, as it did on those of many around him. Over the course of the war, when the world had bigger things on its plate than hitting a little ball into a slightly bigger hole, only ten majors were played out of a possible 24 – he won three of them, and finished top three in all but a couple of the others.

When the guns were finally lowered, Nelson was still just 33 years old and primed to add to his five major victories, but instead he retired the next year to become a rancher. A two-time Masters champion, he continued to play in that tournament and, most years, that tournament alone each year until 1966, and while he finished in the top eight every year up until 1951, he never added another victory.

A great career, no doubt, and one which could have been even better were it not for a couple of global catastrophes – but where is the anomaly?

It came in 1945, an historic year for many reasons, most notably the suicide of one of history's great dictators and the conclusion of one of history's great wars. A lesser-known occurrence from the same year was Byron Nelson winning 11 consecutive PGA tournaments, and 18 in total throughout the year – both records which still stand by a pretty hefty margin over 75 years later.

The year started well for him. He finished in the top two in its first eight tournaments, though he was forced to settle for second on five of those occasions. In the ninth tournament of the year he endured a comparatively disappointing sixth-place finish, but he bounced back in kind at the Miami International Four-Ball tournament, where he and Jug McSpaden swept through the field to help Nelson to his fourth victory of the year – and what would be the start of a famous streak.

As an aside: including a team match-play victory in the streak may seem like an attempt to glorify the achievement, but it was a PGA tournament and is always included in the record – and even if it were omitted, the ten in a row that Nelson won after it would comfortably be the most in history regardless.

He followed that up with a playoff win at the Charlotte Open, an eight-stroke victory at the Greater Greensboro Open, a five-stroke win in Durham and a nine-stroke win in Atlanta. A six-week hiatus ensued, with Nelson sitting on a five-tournament winning streak – already a record at the time. At this point, the streak was beginning to garner the attention of the public – not an easy thing to do in a time where the headlines tended to centre around war instead of golf. As Nelson himself put it, the pressure was beginning to build.

The break did nothing to slow his momentum. Nelson won the first tournament back – in Montreal in early June – by a massive ten shots, then went to Philadelphia and snuck over the line in a tight contest by just two.

The streak continued in Chicago, but the whole situation was beginning to take its toll. Not only had Nelson suffered a back injury during his eighth consecutive victory, but the weight of expectation was starting to get on his nerves. According to the man himself, he told his wife Louise one night during a tournament that he wished he could just get the whole thing over with – the next day he went out and shot 66.

His ninth win came in the only official major tournament of the year, the PGA Championship, before he cantered home at the Tam O'Shanter Open to win by 11 strokes. His final win in the streak came at the Canadian Open, which he won by four shots.

At long last, more than five months after Byron Nelson had last entered a PGA tournament which he didn't win, he came fourth at the Memphis Open, and according to him the loss didn't come a moment too soon. He was exhausted.

He bounced back the following week to win the Knoxville International by a lazy ten shots, and won another three throughout the rest of the year to take his season total to 18 tournament victories – out of the 30 that he entered. To non-golfing fans, it might be difficult to grasp the significance of these numbers, but bear in mind that winning a single tournament is an achievement in itself. There were 142 other players who Nelson had to beat just to win the 1945 PGA Championship. For comparison, in the 2020/21 season, four was the most tournaments that any individual player won, while that number goes down to three for the previous couple of seasons. Both of these factors are reminders that a solitary PGA Tour victory takes a fair bit of doing. Winning 11 in a row, and 60% of the tournaments in a year, was unheard of before Nelson's time, and has remained so for the 75 years since.

Unsurprisingly, Tiger Woods tops the list of challengers to Nelson's record-breaking streak. He stands alone in second place with seven wins in a row, which he accomplished over the 2006 and 2007 seasons, and also shares third place with Ben Hogan – they each won six in a row in 1948 and 1999/2000 respectively. Woods and Hogan are also in fifth with five wins. Woods, Hogan and of course Nelson aside, no one else in the history of the PGA Tour has won more than four times in a row, and if you add Jack Burke Jr to the equation no one has won more than three.

GOLF SEASON: BYRON NELSON, 1945

Evidently, even winning three consecutive PGA tournaments is a very uncommon accomplishment, and once you get to four in a row you're in seriously rarefied air, something which the graph below details. In the Tour's history – which stretches back close to 100 years – on only 37 occasions has a player won back-to-back-to-back. 28 of those streaks ended at three wins, while three more ended at four.

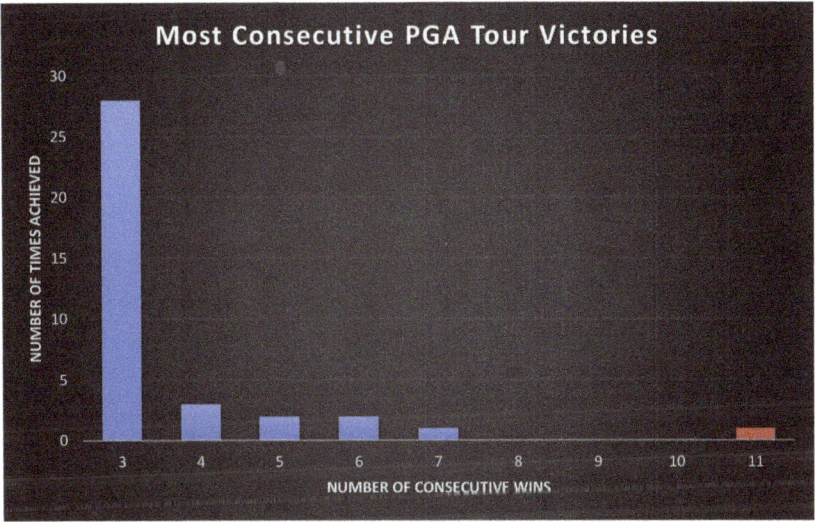

And as for who has come closest to nearing Nelson's record of 18 victories in a season? That one goes to Ben Hogan, who in 1946 – incidentally the year Nelson retired – won 13 times. Another of Nelson's biggest competitors, Sam Snead, owns the third most successful season ever, having won 11 tournaments in 1950, while Hogan's ten wins in 1948 is the only other occasion in which an individual reached double figures in tournament wins in a single season. In PGA history, a player has won at least eight times within a calendar year on just 14 occasions – half of those occasions saw exactly eight wins, while another three saw nine.

SPORT'S GREATEST STATISTICAL ANOMALIES

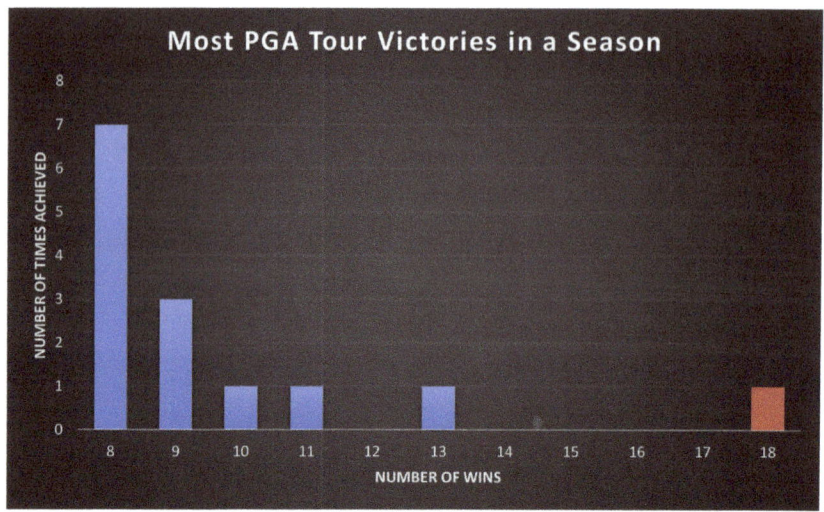

Which brings us to the reasons – aside from the fact that he was a brilliant player – for Nelson's anomaly. Clearly, things were different at the time. The fact that the top four individual seasons in the game's history all came within five years of one another is testament to that.

Nowadays, the best golfers in the world earn millions and millions of dollars in a single year – and that's not counting sponsorships, appearances and any other ways they earn a bit of extra coin to add on that eighth bedroom to their holiday house, or buy a third mega yacht. In contrast, Nelson had to battle away as arguably the best player in the world for over a decade just to buy his ranch. Tiger could probably have bought a handful of ranches every year since the mid '90s.

These lower earning numbers mean that, invariably, there was a much smaller pool of talent. Unlike today, there were probably only a select few people growing up who dreamt of slogging it out on tour to make a meagre living – particularly given the array of other issues plaguing the world at the time – meaning Nelson wouldn't have been facing the depth of competition back then as the best in the world do today.

This was exacerbated further still by the fact that many players were engaged in wartime duties throughout 1945. This would have taken away a lot of competitors, a number of whom could have reduced Nelson's success rate throughout the course of the year. Though there were plenty of good players around, by far his two biggest rivals at the time were Sam Snead and Ben Hogan. Snead still managed to play in a large proportion of tournaments that season – 28 in total, and seven of the 11 that Nelson won in succession. Hogan, on the other hand, widely regarded as one of the best to ever play the game, played in just 18 tournaments during the year and only *two* during Nelson's streak.

So there were some mitigating factors which contributed to both his incredible year and his incredible streak, and the scoring averages from that year also suggest that the season, incredible though it was, may not have ended up as statistically anomalous as it did had it taken place in another era. In the 30 tournaments he entered in 1945, Nelson averaged 68.33 strokes per round. That number has been bettered on one occasion – by Tiger Woods in 2000, when he averaged 68.17.

Of course, raw numbers are a pretty rudimentary way to analyse golf scores given the array of variables which occur even day-to-day, let alone tournament-to-tournament and era-to-era. Nowadays, an 'adjusted scoring average' – which alters the raw numbers based on the performance of the rest of the field – is typically used to nullify these variables, but unfortunately that stat wasn't around in wartime, so we're stuck with 68.33 as the measuring stick for Nelson's year.

But while it may not be a perfect comparison, the fact that Tiger bettered this number in a season in which he won only half as many tournaments as Nelson did in 1945 is perhaps testament to the mitigating factors highlighted above. So too is the fact that in that same year, Tiger played in only 20 tournaments – had he played a full season, he could easily have won more and destroyed this entire chapter.

It is worth noting, however, that throughout the course of 1945 Nelson's final round average sat at a very impressive 67.68. Many of the tournaments Nelson won throughout that famous year came in comprehensive circumstances, so these low scoring final rounds weren't always required, but on a few occasions he was also forced to perform at the tail end of numerous events to keep the streak going. In just the second tournament of the streak, the Charlotte Open, he was tied with Snead after four rounds, and the two came back the next day for an 18-hole playoff. They were again tied after that round, so he had to come out again and beat Snead to the tune of four strokes in the second 18-hole playoff. Then, after six consecutive wins and with the streak well and truly in the public eye, Nelson had to pull out a final round 63 to steal the Philadelphia Inquirer by just two shots.

Clearly, it was an extraordinary run of form. Equally as clearly, however, there were some extenuating circumstances at play. It's always difficult to compare sports across different eras and numbers which meant one thing 70 years ago might not necessarily mean the same thing today, and it's hard to argue that this isn't the case with Nelson's 1945 season. A number of factors combined to make the probability of one player dominating the tour much higher, and it's for that reason that it's unlikely that Nelson's records from 1945 will ever be broken.

But despite these factors, nothing will take away from the fact that it's one of the greatest individual seasons in sporting history. Yes, Nelson might have had a little help from World War II, but he was still playing in the best tour in the world against most of the best players in the world, and he smoked them – 11 times in a row.

By the Numbers

- In 1945, Nelson won **11 consecutive PGA tournaments**; no other player has won more than **7 in a row**.

- Only **9 times in PGA history** has a player **won 4 or more PGA tournaments in succession**.

- That same year, Nelson won a total of **18 PGA tournaments**; the **second most in a calendar year is 13**, and only **2 players aside from Nelson** have won **10 or more** in a year.

13

Ice Hockey Career: Wayne Gretzky

WAYNE GRETZKY DOESN'T look like an athlete. He stands at a very average 6'0", maxed out at a mediocre 84kg during his playing days, and – at least when he didn't have a pair of skates on – possessed a thoroughly ordinary level of athleticism. Despite this, he was able to forge a career as unequivocally the greatest ice hockey player of all time over the course of the last two decades of the 20th century, relying largely on, well, basically everything aside from his size.

During his glittering career, he won the Hart Memorial Trophy as the most valuable player in the league on nine occasions; no one else has managed more than six, and only two other players have won it more than three times. Even more incredibly, those nine wins came in just ten seasons, and he won it eight consecutive times between 1979/80 and 1986/87. Throughout nearly the entirety of the 1980s, Wayne Gretzky winning the Hart Memorial Trophy was virtually a lay down misère.

Gretzky could quite literally do it all. He had an uncanny ability to read the game, setting up teammates with a regularity nobody has ever matched, often from behind the net in an area which has for years been known as 'Gretzky's office'. Of course, an ability to read the play means nothing without the ability to execute, and with well over 1.5 times more assists than anyone else in NHL history, it's safe to say that he had both. From a physical standpoint, while his size was nothing to write home about, he was renowned for his otherworldly stamina, and his effortless, athletic skating was a feature of his game in spite of his lack of obvious natural physical gifts.

Stature aside, there wasn't much missing from Gretzky's game, and throughout his illustrious 20 seasons at the top level, he used this raft of attributes to compile the best career in NHL history by a country mile, and one of the best in the history of sport.

Like with other athletes who enjoyed anomalously dominant career such as Bradman, it's hard to pinpoint exactly how on earth he became so much better than everyone else. Was Gretzky always destined for greatness; a proverbial freak of nature? Or was his incomparable ability on the ice a product of his upbringing – making him a freak of nurture, I suppose. Presumably there was a healthy amount of natural aptitude coursing through Gretzky's veins, but the fact that he was essentially brought up on ice would no doubt have helped him to capitalise on his exceptional innate talents.

In 1961, seven months after he was born in Brantford, Ontario, Gretzky's family moved into a house in which they chose to live in part because it had a backyard they could use as a makeshift ice rink during the winter. It turns out that was a pretty good decision by parents Phyllis and Walter, because that ice rink would be where a young Wayne, who would later come to be known as The Great One, honed his skating skills as a youngster.

It was clear from a very young age that he had a decent dose of natural talent. By the age of six he was playing with ten-year-olds, and not only that, he was far better than them. By 13 he was apparently being booed in his local pee-wee tournament – always a sign that you're doing something right – and to both get away from those interesting individuals booing a child playing sport and in an attempt to further his career, his family moved to Toronto.

At 17 years of age, Gretzky joined the Indianapolis Racers in the World Hockey Association, which was at the time in competition with the National Hockey League. Competition between the two leagues, however, was not exactly fierce, with the NHL widely regarded as the higher quality league. Just 25 games into that first and only season, the Racers folded and Gretzky's contract was sold to the Edmonton Oilers, and at the conclusion of the season the league folded. An inauspicious start to his career to say the least.

Despite the hurdles, however, Gretzky had enjoyed a successful first year personally, finishing third in the league in points (points in ice hockey, for those who are unaware, are evaluated by combining a player's goal and assist totals) and helping his team to the finals. His Edmonton Oilers would fortunately go on to join the NHL the following year, but whether the success of the slightly built teenager would translate to the more competitive league remained to be seen.

It did. In his first year in the NHL, Gretzky tied with Marcel Dionne for first in scoring with 137 points – at the time the fourth most in league history. It was also, and still is, the highest scoring rookie season ever, and was sufficient to earn the 19-year-old Gretzky the first of his eight successive MVP awards.

The year after, he broke the scoring record pretty comfortably with 164 points – the previous highest tally in a season was 152. The year after that, he managed 92 goals and 120 assists for a total of 212 points – 60 (and close to 1.4 times) more than anyone other than himself had ever accumulated in a season.

He would ultimately only better this 212-point total on one occasion, but he managed to pass 200 four times in all – no one else has done it even once. Mario Lemieux got to 199 in the 1988-89 season, but fortunately for the aforementioned statistic he couldn't manage a 200th point – 'the only player to score 201 or more points' doesn't quite have the same ring to it.

Speaking of statistics without a ring to them – by the end of his career, Gretzky had accumulated nine seasons with 163 points or more, something which, to this day, no one except for Lemieux – who has done it twice – has achieved at all. In fact, Lemieux and Gretzky aside, the highest scoring total in a single season is a comparably insignificant 155 by Steve Yzerman.

The graph below plots every individual season in which a player scored 130 points or more in a season – something which had happened on 49 occasions at the time of writing. Gretzky is responsible for 13 of them, including the top four and nine of the top 11.

ICE HOCKEY CAREER: WAYNE GRETZKY

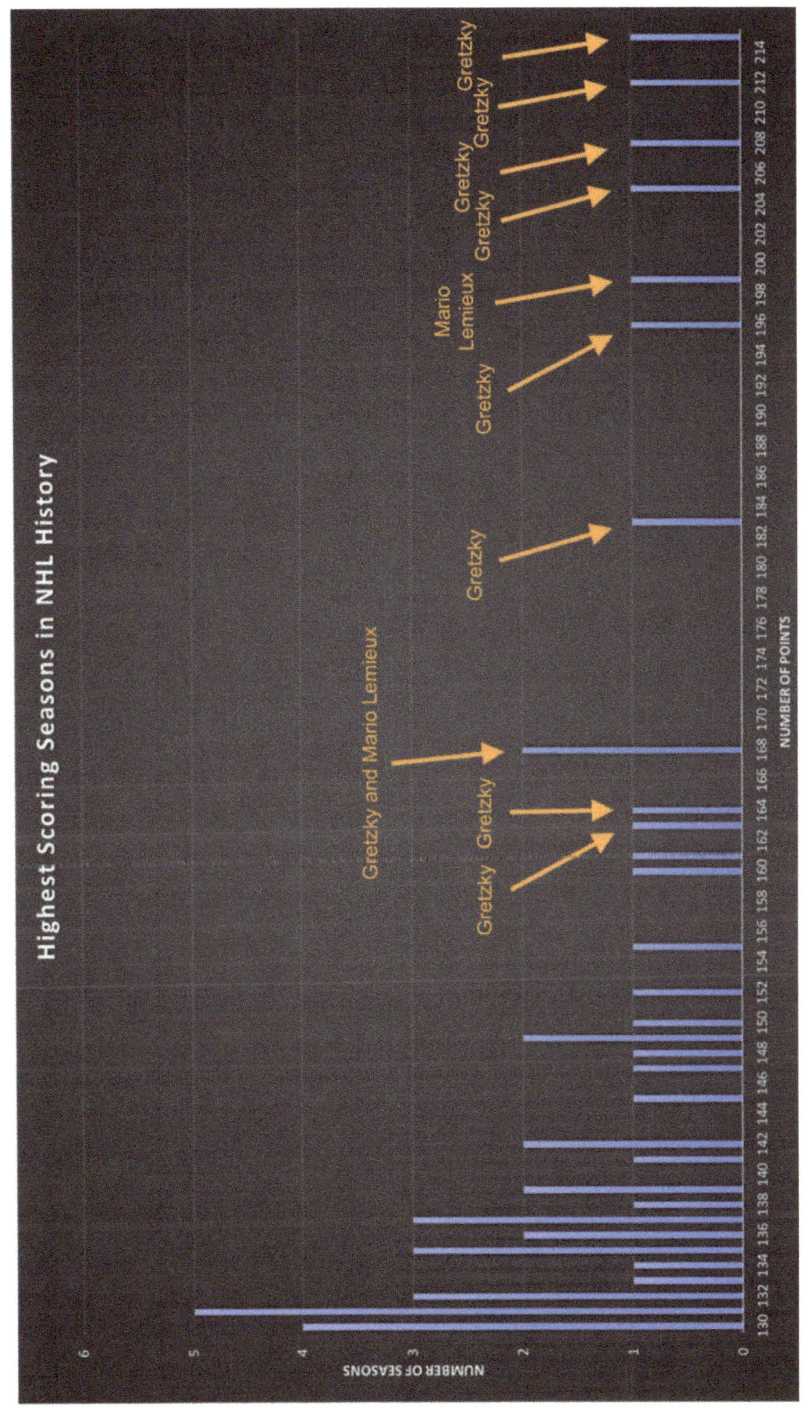

As you can see, Wayne Gretzky has done a pretty good job of taking ownership of the right-hand side of this graph. Funnily enough, Lemieux would probably have a place in this book himself if it weren't for the existence of Gretzky, but even he can't do a whole lot to take away The Great One's historical statistical dominance.

At his best, Gretzky was clearly the best to ever play the game, but courtesy of a relatively injury-free career he was also able to play at a high level for a long time. He managed to accumulate 100 or more points in 13 consecutive seasons – the record for the next most successive seasons in triple figures is shared by Lemieux, Yzerman, Bobby Orr, Mike Bossy, Peter Stastny and Guy Lafleur. They had six.

Unsurprisingly, his dominance combined with his longevity mean that Gretzky's overall career numbers are pretty damn good, and it's in those numbers that he's more easily able to dispose of Lemieux and stand alone as one of sport's biggest statistical outliers.

The below graph includes the top 20 scorers in NHL history, as of the conclusion of the 2021/22 regular season. The blue in each data point refers to assists accumulated throughout each player's career, while the orange relates to goals. As is consistently mentioned in adulations of Gretzky's career, his assist numbers alone would be enough to see him the highest scorer in NHL history, with his blue tower just poking its head over the entire buildings constructed by the likes of Jaromir Jagr and Mark Messier.

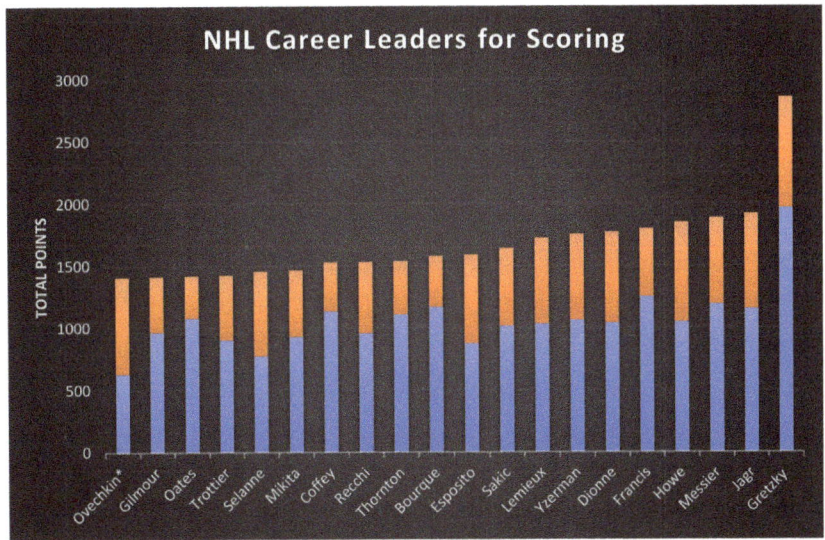

As you can see, when his goals are added to the equation, his tower looks completely out of place, with his total career points an extraordinary 1.487 times that of second-placed Jagr.

Sometimes these kinds of statistics can be misleading, because career totals are not just a product of performance – they're also a product of how long a player has played. Often, players have great career statistics largely as a product of their longevity. Without wanting to dismiss the importance of that, I do think people sometimes forget to factor in how good a player was throughout the course of a career. Some players end up with fantastic career stats despite only being a decent player purely because they played for a long time, and while that doesn't mean they don't deserve acclaim, it also doesn't change the fact that they were only a decent player.

Gretzky played for a pretty long time, but as the first graph in this chapter showed, he was also by far the most dominant player the game has seen throughout his 20 year-career. And in fact, though his 20-year, 1487-game career was a long one, eight of the players who enjoy a spot in the top-20 in career points played more games than Gretzky. Indeed, the four players immediately to his left in the above graph happen to all sit in the top five in the career games record list – Gretzky comes in at 24th.

None of these numbers – games played, points or assists scored – include playoffs, but unsurprisingly that wouldn't have changed much except to give Gretzky an even bigger lead. The winner of four Stanley Cups, he had a pretty prominent playoff career, and his 382 playoff points leads Mark Messier in second with 295. Jari Kurri is in third with 233, a little over 60% of Gretzky's total.

I always think the most impressive outliers are those which relate to an entire career. Don Bradman would be one such example, Gretzky another. That's not to discredit the efforts of the likes of Wilt Chamberlain for his 1961/62 season or Byron Nelson's exploits in 1945, but that Gretzky was able to forge an entire career which was so much better than any other ice hockey players in history is super impressive. Maybe that's unfair, because Chamberlain and Nelson are competing against every other season ever played in the history of basketball while Gretzky and Bradman are only (only being a relative term) competing against every other career, but to me it just feels more impressive, and is certainly more closely tied to someone being the best ever at their given sport.

Having said that, one thing that Gretzky has which Bradman doesn't is a challenger to the throne. While Bradman was so far and away ahead of everyone else that comparisons are not even worth the time it takes to type them, Gretzky has Lemieux sitting perhaps not on his heels, but a couple of strides back as the second most statistically successful ice hockey player of all time. Clearly Gretzky was the most productive player ever and did it for a long time, but Lemieux could potentially have at least closed the gap if he was able to get on the rink a little more. Gretzky's points per game total of 1.92 (during regular season games) is the best ever, but it's almost matched by Lemieux's 1.88. Lemieux, however, played more than 500 games less, hence why he finds himself in a measly eighth in career points. At this point, Gretzky's longevity at least relative to probably his nearest competitor as the greatest of all time helps to explain, to an extent, how he accumulated so many more points than anyone else.

But alas, Lemieux didn't play those 500 extra games, and even if he did, while he would have built an impressive tower on the above graph, it's unlikely to have matched Gretzky. And Lemieux aside, no other player got even close to Gretzky for production per game. Nobody else has ever managed even 1.5 points per game, with Mike Bossy sitting in third place with a 1.497 average. This innocuous-looking man from Ontario has had just one person go even close to matching him for in per-game productivity in over 100 years of NHL history.

Few dominant players in any sport haven't had both a natural aptitude for their game and an upbringing conducive to fostering that talent. Gretzky was no exception, but like Bradman, he was just one of those rare species who managed to develop into a significantly better player at his chosen sport than anyone else in history. He forged a career unparalleled in quality, and by combining that with a pretty decent dose of quantity, he accumulated statistics that don't appear likely to ever be matched.

By the Numbers

- Gretzky scored **2,857 points** (goals + assists) in his NHL career; **1.487 times** that of second-placed Jaromir Jagr, who had **1,921**.

- He owns the **top 4 highest scoring seasons** in NHL history in terms of points, as well as **6 of the top 7** and **9 of the top 11**.

- Gretzky totalled **more assists** than anyone else has ever totalled in **assists and goals combined.**

14

Squash Career: Heather McKay

UNLESS YOU WERE a squash enthusiast in the '60s and '70s, there's a good chance you haven't heard of Heather McKay. And yet, for all her relative anonymity, she owns the precious title of being the most statistically successful player in the history of her sport, and by some margin.

It's not often that someone with such a long list of sporting achievements is so unknown, but testament to just how far under the radar McKay has flown throughout her life is the difficulty with which I found relevant information for this chapter. There is astonishingly little available to read about someone who is unequivocally the most successful person in her field in history – particularly given that field is a sport.

There are a few contributing factors to this, not least that squash is not exactly in the top echelon of sports in terms of global popularity, but regardless – given that you'd struggle to find someone with as much sustained success as she had in the history of any sport, a little more press would probably be warranted.

Despite all this success, McKay's squash career didn't actually begin until the age of 19 after a childhood in which it played virtually no part. She hailed from a competitive sporting family, but her and her ten siblings were more focused on golf, rugby, tennis and hockey to bother with squash. McKay herself was quite talented at the latter two, and it wasn't until the age of 17 that she first gave squash a passing thought – and even then, that was only to reap the fitness benefits it would sow and improve her performance on the hockey field.

A few short years later she was the best squash player on the planet, a title she wouldn't relinquish for close to 20 years. In 1960, she began her career by winning the Australian Amateur Championship. Later that year she lost in the quarterfinals of the New South Wales Championship to Yvonne West, a noteworthy moment because it marked the first of two times in her competitive career that she would lose a match. The second came at the Scottish Open in 1962 against Fran Marshall, and for the remaining 19 years of her professional sporting life it didn't happen again.

The most quantifiable way to measure her success – if it isn't obvious enough from the fact that she didn't lose for almost 20 years – is to look at the British Open, at the time the most prestigious tournament in world squash, and still viewed that way by many. She first won it in 1962, and continued winning it every year until 1978, when she stepped away to let some other players have a turn.

Though there have been a number of dominant squash players throughout the sport's history – perhaps a product of the fact that there just aren't as many competitors as there are in more mainstream sports – none have got close to the 16 consecutive British Opens McKay managed throughout the '60s and '70s, nor even the 16 total that she won. The below graph shows how McKay's success at the event compares to her competitors for the crown of best squash player in history.

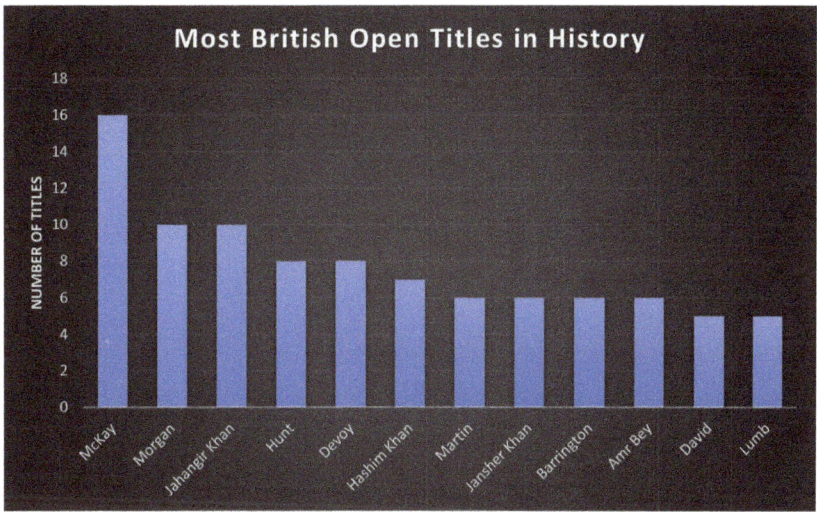

Britain's Janet Morgan is the closest on the women's side – she won every British Open in the '50s for her ten titles – while for the men, Pakistan's Jahangir Khan also won ten in total and ten in a row from 1982 to 1991.

But they fall well short of 16, and even within their victories they didn't enjoy the kind of dominance that McKay did. That's not to diminish the feat of winning the most prestigious tournament in your chosen sport ten consecutive times, but she set a high standard.

A quick background on the scoring system in professional squash: the sport employs a best-of-five games system, with the winner of a game being the first to nine points – at least that's been the case throughout much of squash's history. In recent years that's flitted around to 15 and 11 points a little bit, and it was also first-to-11 in the women's game in the early 1920s, but the vast majority of British Opens have been played to nine.

Jahangir Khan and Janet Morgan won plenty of their finals in three games, and often three pretty comfortable games, but they did drop a few over the course of their dominance.

During her 16-year winning streak at the British Open, McKay didn't lose a single game in a final – in fact she only lost two games at the tournament at all during that time – and in nine of her 16 finals lost five points or less in the entire match. In 1968 she enjoyed a 9-0, 9-0, 9-0 win against Bev Johnson which lasted 15 minutes, literally the time it takes to drink a coffee. The next year she won 9-2, 9-0, 9-0, the year after it was 9-1, 9-1, 9-0…you get the picture. They weren't all as dominant as that, but over the 16 years her finals opponents averaged less than seven points per match.

The below graph compares McKay with other dominant performers at the tournament on the basis of the average number of points they conceded to their opponents in finals at the tournament. The graph includes every player on both the men's and women's side who has won at least six British Open Championships. It's a fairly arbitrary number which includes five men and four women but to be honest, the average points against in finals for those who have won less than six gets so far from McKay it's not even worth worrying about.

SQUASH CAREER: HEATHER MCKAY

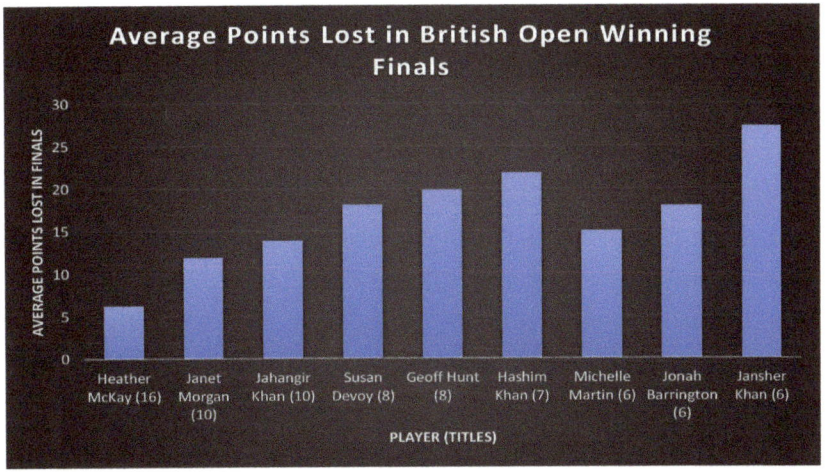

The players are ordered from left to right in terms of how many titles they won. As you can see, McKay's little building sits at a little over 6 – 6.25 to be exact. That means that in an average final she would have won roughly 9-2, 9-2, 9-2. Her rivals aren't particularly close. Janet Morgan sits in second with a very impressive average points conceded of 11.9, but even this is nearly double that of McKay. Most of these players conceded closer to three times that of McKay. I should mention that poor old Jansher Khan had to deal with playing first-to-15 in his last three titles, which skews his numbers a little, but given he lost more points in the finals of his first two titles than McKay did in her last ten it's safe to say he wouldn't have been particularly close regardless.

It's worth bearing in mind that this is not a graph of McKay compared against other average squash players. It's her performance relative to the most successful players in the game's history. They are extraordinary numbers, and have her well and truly in the conversation of the most dominant sportspeople in history.

So how did she get there? It's safe to say a good amount of talent was involved, but she also boasted a work ethic unparalleled in the sport's professional ranks at the time. According to McKay, her husband often used the phrase, "If you don't do the training don't do the complaining," and McKay cites this mindset as giving her the confidence that she could overcome her opponent when mired in what she termed a "hum dinger of a match". The irony of that is that the vast majority of her victories came with such ease that a large element of her conditioning rarely had a chance to be truly relevant. And so while this superior fitness no doubt played a role in her ability to win with such regularity, that she so often avoided these so-called hum dingers suggests that talent probably played more of a role than anything else.

There is, of course, also the reality – without wanting to be disparaging – that professional squash in the '60s and '70s probably didn't possess the kind of depth of talent that we see in many sports today. It's possible that the extraordinary streaks she managed to put together wouldn't have existed if there was a little more competition. The sport was still developing while she was playing it. This is certainly not something exclusive to squash – a number of the achievements recognised in this book likely wouldn't have occurred under the same conditions in the modern world simply because there is more of a bottleneck of talent in professional sport today.

Indeed, a quick look at the British Open winners over the years reveals this very idea. Between the beginning of the tournament – in 1922 for women and 1930 for men – and the turn of the millennium, eight men and six women won it at least four times in a row. In the first 20 years thereafter, nobody won it more than twice in succession. If all things were equal, McKay probably wouldn't be able to win 16 in a row in the modern game – but having said that, nor would most of the people who got remotely close to matching her feat have been able to win ten in a row, or eight in a row.

McKay's resume also boasts victories at the first two Women's World Championships, the first of which came in 1976. At that stage she still had a British Open or two left in her, but her playing commitments were dwindling and she was living in Canada, devoting a significant portion of her time to coaching. Regardless, she won the first incarnation of the tournament courtesy of a 9-2, 9-2, 9-0 victory in the final. The tournament wasn't played over the next two years, during which time McKay won her 16th and final British Open, but she returned to compete for another World Championship in 1979 despite having stepped away from other major events. At almost 40 years of age and somewhat out of practice she could have been forgiven for being a little rusty, but she quickly squashed any doubts about who was the best player in the world. She did, in fact, lose the first game of the final in that tournament before going on to win 6-9, 9-3, 9-1, 9-4, so perhaps by her standards that was an indication that her career was coming to a close.

McKay played a significant role in helping develop the women's game, and a couple of years after her retirement the Women's International Squash Players Association came into existence, marking a major development for women's squash. The creation of this association helped to shape an increasingly competitive landscape, and while McKay wasn't around to prove her worth as the depth of competition grew, she had competed against many of the women who were – and she beat them like she was shooting fish in a barrel.

The sport might not have been as competitive as it is today, but there were still plenty of other extremely talented players, and none of them could beat her – none could even get close. She was so far and away better than everyone else she ever played against that not only did she not lose for 19 years, she rarely played a game in which she didn't completely annihilate her opponent. It might not be a mainstream sport, but it's possible that no other sportsperson in history has been so dominant in his or her field as Heather McKay.

Testament to her sporting prowess, McKay also represented Australia at a national level in a couple of other sports, as you do. In 1967 and 1971, a few years into her career atop world squash, she represented Australia in field hockey, which as you may remember was the sport that she was trying to accumulate a little bit of fitness for when she first took up squash. She was also pretty handy at racquetball, and is now a member of the Hall of Fame for that sport.

There's no doubt that there were a number of mitigating factors which probably made it more likely for one squash player to stand out significantly from the rest during McKay's career – or at least one major factor. Without wanting to denigrate her opponents, it's hardly surprising that a non-mainstream sport 50 or 60 years ago wouldn't have been nearly as competitive as most sports are today. McKay, however, took it to the point where it's hard not to laud her supremacy. The door might have been ajar for someone to dominate, but she swung it off its hinges.

By the Numbers

- McKay **lost just 2 matches** in her career, and was undefeated for the **last 19 years** of it.

- She won a total of **16 British Opens** in a row; no one else has won **more than 10**.

- McKay conceded an average of just **6.25 points** in British Open finals – Janet Morgan has the second best record for this statistic, conceding an average of **11.9 points**, nearly **twice that of McKay**, while Jahangir Khan is third conceding an average of **13.9 points**.

15

Basketball Team: The Boston Celtics, 1950s and '60s

WINNING EVERY CHAMPIONSHIP for close to a decade is an incredible feat in any sporting league, but it's not entirely unheard of for a team to enjoy such a prolonged period of success. The North Carolina Tar Heels women's soccer team won nine consecutive national championships in the 1980s and '90s, Žalgiris won the Lietuvos krepšinio lyga (Lithuanian Basketball League) 11 times in a row between 2011 and 2021, and there are countless other examples of leagues in which one team has dominated over an extended period. Generally, however, such streaks are a little more elusive in the biggest leagues of most sports around the globe. For the most part, the NBA has exemplified this fact, and in the first 75 years of the league, winning more than three successive titles proved a bridge too far for virtually all of the NBA's great teams. The Lakers couldn't manage it during any of their extended runs, nor could Michael Jordan's irrepressible Bulls of the '90s or the revolutionary Warriors of recent years. There has, however, been one exception.

In 1959, the Celtics swept the team which was then known as the Minneapolis Lakers 4-0 in the NBA Finals to earn their second NBA championship – and their second in three years. In 1960, they won again. Then they won the next year, and the next, and the next, and the next, and the next, and the next. For those of you not keeping count, that's eight in a row – five more than any other team has ever managed, even over half a century later. Incidentally, after losing in the Eastern Conference Finals to Wilt Chamberlain's 76ers the next season, they won in 1968 and 1969 to round out the greatest dynasty in the history of the league, and one of the greatest ever in sport.

It must have been a frustrating time to be a fan of the league, unless of course you were from Massachusetts. Between 2015 and 2018, Golden State won three championships in four seasons and you would have been excused for thinking it spelled the end of competitive sport as we know it such was the violent reaction from fans around the globe. One shudders to imagine how today's world of anonymous Twitter comments and Facebook insults would have dealt with a team winning every year for almost an entire decade.

At the time, however, it probably didn't seem quite as unusual as it does when reflecting on it today. The first of the Celtics' eight consecutive championships came in just the league's 12th year, so there really hadn't been much time for any trends to develop. Since their reign ended, however, a continual lack of any team putting its collective hand up to break the mould and challenge the Celtics' streak has painted it in an even greater light with every passing year.

The graph below details every NBA championship since the league started back in 1947. Successive championships won by the same

BASKETBALL TEAM: THE BOSTON CELTICS, 1950S AND '60S

team are piled up on top of each other, and once a new team is crowned the count goes back to one. The bar correlating to 1950, for example, represents the second consecutive championship won by the Minneapolis Lakers, hence the bar reaches two on the y-axis, before jumping back to one when the Rochester Royals won the year after.

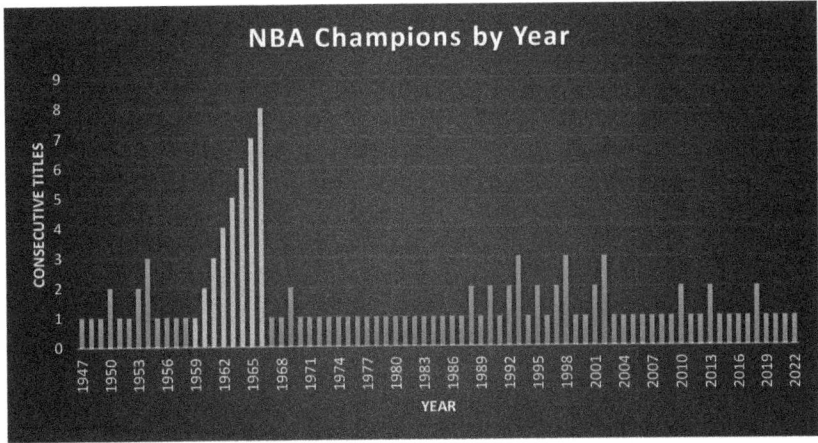

As you can see, the vast majority of championship teams have been unable to back it up the next year. In fact, on only 13 occasions in the NBA's first 76 years did a team win consecutive championships – that's out of 53 opportunities. And of those 13 streaks, eight finished at two, four more at three, and of course way out on top, the Celtics' at eight.

As the graph demonstrates, there have been periods where consecutive titles were more common. The Lakers team of the late '80s kickstarted a period of 16 years in which just a solitary team – the Spurs in '99 – didn't go back-to-back, and three more teams managed the double soon thereafter. It's a far cry from the '70s and the bulk of the '80s, during which the graph resembles a paddock and teams were booted from their proverbial throne faster than you can say Bill Russell.

Back in the '60s, it's hard to say whether it would have been common or not for teams to win back-to-back, because the Celtics won virtually all of the titles. In the 12 seasons prior to their eight-year streak, seven championship teams failed to win the next year, while the Minneapolis Lakers had two streaks (of two and three respectively). Following the Celtics' reign, as mentioned, no team won multiple championships until 1987, with the exception of the Celtics themselves winning two more in a row a year after their streak of eight ended.

It's a truly absurd streak of success and one which would be virtually impossible to fathom happening in today's game. The aforementioned Golden State Warriors achieved their own success by accumulating what felt like an unreasonable amount of the league's talent – partly this was courtesy of drafting, partly free agency. Already they were dominant in 2015 and 2016, establishing themselves as one of the most talented teams in the game's history thanks to their revolutionary backcourt of Stephen Curry and Klay Thompson – even if they lost the 2016 Finals at the hands of LeBron James' Cavaliers – so when they went and added arguably the best player in the world in Kevin Durant prior to the 2016/17 season, the rest of the league was understandably frustrated. They were virtually unstoppable the next two seasons, winning consecutive NBA Finals series first 4-1 and then 4-0, but two years later Durant had left, the dynasty was over and they were one of the worst teams in the league. They did bounce back to win again in 2021/2022, but regardless, for all of their dominance, they won just three NBA championships at the peak of their powers – which already felt like plenty. Eight in a row and 11 in 13 years is hard to imagine.

There were, however, plenty of differences between today's NBA and the version which existed in the 1960s. For starters, there was no free agency, which meant that the rampant player movement which exists in the modern-day NBA wasn't really part of the league. This means that the likes of Kevin Durant wouldn't have been able to leave the side after just a couple of years to go and play with his friends in Brooklyn – though having said that it also means that he wouldn't have been able to join the side as easily in the first place.

But undoubtedly the biggest difference was the fact that back in the '60s, there were only eight teams in the league. Nowadays, assuming all teams are equal, a team has a roughly 1 in 656 billion ($(1 \text{ in } 30)^8$) chance of winning eight titles on the trot, while back then it was closer to 1 in 17 million ($(1 \text{ in } 8)^8$). Eight in a row was still pretty unlikely, but it was much more feasible than it would be today. Perhaps if the Warriors only had seven teams to compete against they would have managed a few more.

Though it was still an extremely unlikely feat, it can't be understated how significant a difference this is, and winning eight consecutive championships in a league with only seven opponents doesn't hold a candle to a similar achievement today. When you add in the fact that levels of professionalism within the league and indeed sport moreover back in the mid 20th century were much lower, the chances of a single team reigning supreme over the rest for such an extended period of time were substantially higher. In stark contrast to today, players in the '60s could have been lighting up in the locker room at half-time and few people would have batted an eyelid, so when an extremely talented team with very high standards of professionalism came along they were invariably a pretty good chance of winning a lot more often than they lost. It's probably a major reason – in fact arguably the predominant reason – that so many anomalies outlined in this book occurred such a long time ago.

But as the old adage goes, you can only beat the teams in front of you, and the Celtics certainly did that. A brief look at their performance over the years also suggests that they were quite comfortably the best team in the league throughout their dynasty – something which probably doesn't come as all that much of a surprise. In the first seven of their eight consecutive titles they were the number one seed, only dropping to number two in 1966, and they also won four of the eight best-of-seven NBA Finals series either 4-1 or 4-0.

Clearly they were a dominant outfit, and the number of regular season wins during their eight consecutive title-winning years shows a predictable but nonetheless significant lead over the rest of their rivals. The graph below illustrates this, along with the fun fact that the Knicks were equally disappointing over half a century ago as they are today.

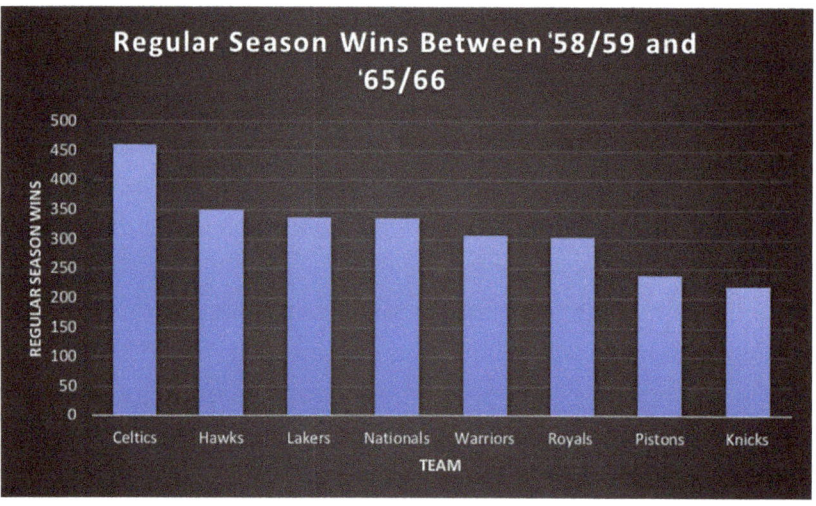

Boston were just as dominant in the playoffs. During these seasons, no other team won more than 50% of their playoff games – the Lakers were closest, winning 44 and losing 46, while the Louisville Hawks weren't far behind with 33 wins and 36 losses. The Celtics won 67 out of 100 for a winning percentage of I guess around 67%.

Their supremacy is plain to see, but despite that there were still a handful of occasions on which their streak could still have ended prematurely. In four of their eight Division Finals during this period, the Celtics needed all seven games in the best-of-seven series to get past their opposition. In total, in only two of these eight seasons did they not require a Game Seven to win either the Division Finals or the Finals themselves. What does this mean? Not much, really, given they won all these games and the championships anyway, but it does show that they weren't completely infallible and needed a hefty number of wins in knockout games to earn this record.

Perhaps the most notable example of this came in 1962, when, in an attempt to win a fourth consecutive title, the Celtics went down 3-2 in the NBA Finals series against the Lakers. In Game 6 they won comfortably to force a decider, and that decider went down to the wire. With the game tied and just a couple of seconds left, Laker Frank Selvy put up a 12-foot attempt to win the championship. It rimmed out, Bill Russell grabbed one of his 40 rebounds for the night and 189 in the series, and the game went to overtime. The Celtics went on to win 110-107.

But as we all know, a hallmark of great teams is an ability to get the job done when it's needed most, and even if they realistically had little to do with Selvy missing his baseline jumper in the dying seconds (there was a good late contest but he was pretty wide open), miss it he did, and the rest is history. And while the boys from Beantown undoubtedly benefited from a significantly smaller pool of competition and a less developed league, they did still boast a damn good team.

Bill Russell took centre-stage as their go-to guy and best player, forging out a career which would end with five MVP awards and 12 All-Star appearances. Russell was a good offensive player, but it was at the other end of the court where he was most impactful. He was arguably the best defender the game has ever seen and would be unequivocally the best rebounder in history if it wasn't for longtime rival Wilt Chamberlain.

Widely regarded as one of the best of all time, Russell was the foundation of the Celtics dynasty, but he had plenty of very capable soldiers alongside him. K.C. Jones gave the Celtics a second brilliant defender, while five-time All-Star Sam Jones slotted in as the team's shooting guard for virtually the entirety of their period of dominance, complementing his defensive superstars with a healthy dose of flair and offensive talent. The versatile John Havlichek spent the first half of his 16-season NBA career, which would ultimately go down as one of the best in Celtics history, winning championships like he was shelling peas with Russell and co. Bob Cousy revolutionised the point guard position playing alongside Russell in the early '60s while his backcourt partner Bill Sharman simultaneously revolutionised the shooting guard spot, Tom Heinsohn was a key cog in the first half of the dominant decade as a player before enjoying a successful career as both a coach and a commentator, Don Nelson played an important albeit less notable role in the latter stages of their dominance, and the list goes on.

And then there was the coach, Red Auerbach. In charge of the Celtics from 1950 until 1966, he played a major role in the acquisition of the likes of Russell and the subsequent composition of the dynastic team, and instilled the defensive intensity which was such a hallmark of their success. With nine championships, Auerbach was comfortably the most successful coach in the league's history for a long time until Phil Jackson came along and won 11. He is perhaps most renowned for his ability to forge great relationships with his players, but he was also a super competitive guy. According to K.C. Jones, Auerbach would "cheat and be foaming at the mouth" when the group would play racquetball, and this manic competitivity must have rubbed off on his team, because during their eight-year streak they won 528 of their 726 games.

His coaching career concluded at the end of the 1965/66 season, in which the Celtics won their eighth consecutive title and their fourth in five years against the Los Angeles Lakers. The following year the streak ended, though with Bill Russell as player-coach the side would go on to win two more in succession in '68 and '69.

It was an incredible streak of success – the greatest in NBA history and one of the greatest in sports – and it will almost certainly never be broken. Even if the stars somehow aligned to make it possible, the modern-day sports world simply wouldn't allow it. Can you imagine the uproar if the Warriors had kept winning until 2024? A competitive league is the foundation of popularity and popularity is the foundation of financial success, and in the businesslike world of American sports a one-team league would not be particularly well-received.

And so, Bill Russell and his Celtics teammates will go to their graves knowing they were almost certainly a part of the most successful team in the history of the NBA. There's no doubt there were a couple of mitigating circumstances which make the feat less improbable than it would be today, as well as a lucky shot or two that fell their way along the journey, but few teams win non-stop for close to a decade without a bit of good fortune. One Frank Selvy jump shot could have cut the streak in two and sent them tumbling to mediocrity as just another team with a couple of consecutive titles, but thankfully for anomaly lovers, the rims were screwed in tight that day.

By the Numbers

- The Celtics won **8 consecutive championships** between 1959 and 1966; no other team has ever won more than **3 in a row**. They also won **10 of 11** up until 1969.

- Only **13 times in the first 75 years** of the NBA did a team win back-to-back championships.

- Between '59 and '66, the Celtics won **461 regular season games**; the second best-performed team was the **Hawks with 350.**

About the Author

JAMES SALMON STUMBLED the world of writing in his mid-20s while travelling the world, eager to make a couple of extra bucks to fund his adventurous/aimless lifestyle. With a Master of Business (Sport Management) under his belt, writing didn't exactly align with his qualifications, and wasn't initially intended to be anything more than a part-time gig. By leaning into his passion for sport, however, he was able to steadily grow his one-man business, and a few years down the track, it's now his full-time job.

James has written on a wide variety of sports for many different publications, including local newspapers and an array of different sporting outlets. He's also worked as a copywriter for companies ranging from Vodafone to local furniture stores, with these roles providing plenty of practice writing on excruciatingly dry topics – after trying to produce engaging copy about wicker chairs, sports statistics felt like a walk in the park. On top of that, he's also worked for several years as an editor for *Ultimate World Publishing* – the publishers of this very book – helping over 50 first-time authors accomplish their goal of writing a book.

A footy fanatic, cricket connoisseur, basketball buff and surfing savant, James' love for sport has always been accompanied by a keen interest in statistics. That interest has lent itself to an inordinate amount of knowledge about fundamentally useless facts and figures, and it's from there that the idea of this book was born.

www.ingramcontent.com/pod-product-compliance
Lightning Source LLC
Chambersburg PA
CBHW041307110526
44590CB00028B/4275